Celebrating the TOO MUCH WOMAN

Celebrating the TOO MUCH WOMAN

We shine because baby, you just can't dim the sun

Gina Hatzis

Gina Hatzis

Copyright © 2019 Gina Hatzis

The moral right of the author has been asserted.

All rights reserved.
No part of this publication may be reproduced, stored in a retrieval system, or transmitted, in any form or by any means, without the prior permission in writing of the publisher, nor be otherwise circulated in any form of binding or cover other than that in which it is published and without a similar condition including this condition being imposed on the subsequent purchaser.

Published by Gina Hatzis

ISBN 978-0-578-46736-8

Typesetting services by BOOKOW.COM

Dedication

This book is lovingly dedicated to the female lineage who grace my family tree.

It begins with my mother, Mary Ann, who has always been the strong, solid trunk of my being.

My grandmothers Constantina and Eftihia, your names remind me to root myself in resilience and joy.

And to all of the Too Much Women who came before me, I sit on these beautiful branches, strengthened by the stories of your lives and nourished by the love running through the veins of our ancestral roots. Seeded deep in my heart and my work, I carry your dreams and desires. May they be honoured in your memory, and may your legacy live on in the fulfilled lives of the future generations to come.

"Every woman who heals herself helps heal all the women who came before her, and all those who come after her." ~Dr. Christiane Northrup

Table of Contents

The Too Much Woman Speech

Why I Wrote This Book

The MOMENT

The MAGIC

How I Got Here

Too Dramatic

Too Sensitive

Too Provocative

Too Voluptuous

Too Complicated

Too Bold

The MOVEMENT

We Are Too Much Women and we will not dim any longer

Sips

My Spiritual G-Spot Excerpt

Acknowledgements

Biography

Social Media

Too Much Woman Speech

What I'm about to say to you might come as a surprise

But the most powerful thing about me baby, is the Thunder of My Thighs

That oh-so-fleshy part of me that forever I've despised.

Has taught me much about My Truth, and teased apart the Lies

See I'm the Too Much Woman and I'm dangerous… can't you see?

My Truth, my Words, my Hips, my Curves

Two handfuls, maybe three!

Too loud, too big, too bold, too wild, too sexy…yeah that's me

And I won't sit down, shut up or dim, tuck it in or hide it away

I won't be taken down a few notches, I won't be shamed, silenced, or put into the corner, baby.

I was born a Too Much little girl in a Big Fat Greek family.

And I was fed compliments along, with second helpings of everything, because food and words are how we loved in my family.

They called me Beauty Queen and Blue-Eyed Princess

And Mmmmm those words tasted as good as Mama's cooking.

I learned early on that My Body was a form of currency.

That with the bat of an eye, a sweet smile, the tilt of my head, I could buy me more love and attention.

And that worked for a while.

Until it didn't.

Until the beauty of my body started to entice customers that I did not want near my store.

So I started to backpedal.

To become small and afraid.

To dim my Too Muchness.

I trained as a dancer and slowly came back to loving my body again.

To feel strong in my skin. Confident in my stride.

And on a crisp fall day in grade nine, I was surrounded by twenty older girls who pinned my arms behind my back – kicking, punching, slapping, spitting…Punishing me for my Too Muchness.

And as the blood dripped from my nose, so did the light in my spirit.

And once again, realizing that I was not safe in my Too Muchness, I dimmed it down.

I spent the next fifteen years teetering cautiously in my Too Much Body.

On the one hand, growing in my womanhood; wanting to be seen and loved and desired.

And on the other hand, so afraid that my body would betray me and invite danger once again.

Fast forward. I am a grown woman. Smart. Educated. Professional.

Delivering a keynote to a sea of over three hundred executive men in suits and deciding *this would be my defining moment.*

Once and for all, I would dare to be seen. Not for my body.

But for my art, for my craft, for what I brought to the table.

So, I manned up!

Serious pants suit, buttoned to the top. Breasts hidden. Hair slicked back into a severe bun. I even bought me some fake glasses.

I dimmed down all the juiciness of my Too Much body and, yeah, I knocked that baby out of the park and flew off the stage to a standing ovation thinking I had finally won the battle by dimming this body down.

And there I was, strolling along in my self-celebration, when I was approached by a man from the audience who asked if he could walk me to my car.

Out in the parking lot, he grabbed my arm. His nails, like talons, digging into my skin.

He pulled me close. Very close. Too close. So close that I could smell the stale coffee and misogyny on his breath as he hissed …"*I have a fetish for librarian types.*"

All I remember is driving. Fast.

Watching my whole life fly past me on the highway and ricochet off the windshield.

The dimming, the tucking, the hiding, the shrinking, the shaming, the dumbing down.

Letting my hair blow wild and the tears flow free, deciding that I would no longer deny my Too Muchness.

From now on, I would dare to be seen in my all-that-juicy-over-the-top-ness.

People carelessly say, "*Love yourself, love your body*", but what they don't say is *"Baby, it's a dangerous game. People will objectify you, they will shun you, they will feel threatened by you, they will criticize you, they will loathe you, they will envy you and they will be afraid of you.*

I say, Yes. All those things, Yes.

But baby, do it anyway.

Eduardo Galeano reminds us that

The Church says this body is a *sin*

Science says this body is a *machine*

Business says this body is a *product*.

But this body says I'm a freaking fiesta!

So, to all the Too Much Woman, I invite you to stand up.

Celebrating the TOO MUCH WOMAN

Stand and be seen in all your Glory.

We are not a piece of human.

We are not flesh and ass and temptation.

We are women.

Connected to our Divinity, our Sensuality, our Life Force Vitality.

We are feminine flow with masculine force.

We are sexy brilliance and hot determination.

We are bigger than our breasts and more powerful than our thighs.

Our curve is mightier than any sword and our wit stronger than any insult.

We do not radiate to taunt you, or tease you, or provoke you, or threaten you.

We shine, not for your adoration.

We shine, because baby, you just can't dim the sun.

Gina xo

Why I wrote this book.

But first... Do you want the *truth*?

I'm seriously asking, because people often *say* they want to hear the truth, and then they hang you for it.

My favourite George Carlin line is, "Everyone appreciates honesty until you're honest with them. Then you're an asshole."

If you want the truth, I'm gonna give it to you.

There's no point starting off this book with some lofty tale about wanting to save the world, the beluga whales, or my tribal sisters, suffering under patriarchal paradigms.

And while I *care deeply* about all of those things, they have very little to do with why I'm sitting here in my spare room at 3:14 am on a frigid Toronto winter morning, banging out this intro.

The truth is, I *didn't* want to write this book. There I said it.

Gasp!

More specifically, this isn't the book I *intended* to write.

See, I have another book that's been in gestation for about a year now, my mini memoir, called *Finding My Spiritual G Spot,* which chronicles my recent journey back to myself, digging into the deeper work and the decisions that ultimately saved my life at 43 years old.

See, that book was supposed to be **The Book**.

I was finally ready to share the massive regrouping that was ignited in August of 2016, when I had my "Come to Jesus Moment" on the **bedroom** floor. (I know the cliché is bathroom floor, but ewww!) The moment itself wasn't that extraordinary, really. I mean, don't most people have a Big Rendering with the God of their Understanding at *some* point in their lives?

When you just can't stand another day living a lie, when your legs buckle under the weight of the façade, and you have to finally admit to *yourself* just how unhappy you are?

When Desperation erratically reaches across from the passenger seat of the car and grabs the steering wheel, swerving maniacally across lanes, barely dodging oncoming traffic, less concerned with safety than with the anguish of continuing on the same painful path?

So, anyway, *Finding My Spiritual G Spot*, The Book, was about that experience, and I felt urgency to write it. Not because I had figured out a fail-proof, five-step process that was going to make a massive difference in people's lives, no.

If you need to know anything about me, it's that a) You'll be my B.F.F. if you serve me a dish of fettucini alfredo and b) I don't subscribe to the expert paradigm. I am *not* your guru, your answer, your saviour, and I sure as heck won't lead you to your salvation.

I felt urgency to write that book because I could not contain it any longer. It was like that moment when my daughter was ready to exit the womb and join us all on the outside.

Now, if you're squeamish, skip this next bit, because it's about to get a little graphic here.

There is a moment during a vaginal birth called the Ring of Fire, which perfectly describes the burning sensation felt as the mother's tissue stretches to its maximum capacity around the baby's head.

It's called the Ring of Fire because **that is exactly what it feels like.**

I delivered both my children without pain medication, so, yeh I can testify. I remember pausing in that moment, when the extreme pain pushed me to the cusp of insanity and looking into my midwife's calm eyes.

"Rezvan," I growled, "I *can't*." I literally meant I couldn't do it. I couldn't push. You see, my daughter was my second child, and I knew something about the pain that was about to go down from the experience with my son.

Rezvan didn't flinch or cajole or console me. She simply and calmly responded with, "You *must*."

She was right. Isabella wanted out and there was no going back, no matter how tightly I squeezed my thighs together.

This is how I felt about my story. *Spiritual G Spot*'s birth was non-negotiable. And although it was uncomfortable to explore this most painful time of my life, rather than resist the process and fight against the Ring of Fire, just like the birth of my babies, I knew that what I wanted most was on the other side.

So, I wrote.

And as I did, I grew more excited about what I was discovering about myself. Much like being a mother, writing deepened my self-awareness, and often what I thought I was writing about, turned out to be a greater insight than I'd realized, as I pushed through.

The momentum was building, and the pieces were fitting together. "I'm doing this!" I shouted silently to the book-gods, as I imagined them nodding and blessing my fingers flying across the keyboard.

I felt that I was typing my sanity with each word, each sentence connecting the random pieces of my messed up story and lining up to form the yellow brick road delivering me to the Land of Oz.

So, you see, that was what was *supposed* to happen. *That* book.

But the Universe had other plans, and unbeknownst to me, my life was about to become barely recognizable. A tsunami was about to hit that would shake up and redirect not only my work, my focus and my writing, but my soul.

THE MOMENT

"Interested."

That one word shifted the trajectory of my life when I innocently typed it into a Facebook post in February 2019.

What happened after that can only be summed up as a tsunami in my professional world.

Within months, my life became barely recognizable.

What I have found to be true for myself is that, when a tidal wave hits in one area of my life, it impacts all areas. And this was no different.

Now, I consider myself a pretty good swimmer, but nothing could have prepared me for the current that would suck, drag, overwhelm and propel me the way this one did.

I found myself continuously choking, gagging and gasping for air at certain times, and euphorically riding the crest of a wave at others.

At the end of each day, I would drop into bed, as though violently purged from the mouth of the ocean onto the gritty lap of the beach, mentally exhausted, physically depleted, emotionally seasick, and somehow licking my salty lips with a smile.

Celebrating the TOO MUCH WOMAN

Here's what happened.

I was mindlessly scrolling on Facebook, and something caught my eye. It was a call to fill the final slot in a Toronto-based speaking competition called Speaker Slam. Someone had pulled out of the competition at the last minute and they needed a replacement, fast. Now, at that point, I had never heard of Speaker Slam, or its hosts Dan and Rina. I hadn't participated in a speaking competition since the eighth grade. And I sure as hell had no idea what I was getting myself into, or why I was intrigued to even consider this.

At that point, I had been speaking professionally for 23 years both corporately and publicly, since leaving my short stint as a journalist. I was writing The Book, creating an online program, managing my steady stream of speaking gigs and I didn't have a thing to prove. And I certainly didn't have the luxury of time to add *one more thing* to my already full list. But *something* prompted me to type *Interested*, and put the wheels in motion to pivot my life in a drastic way.

Within moments of typing that one word, I received a Facebook message, a phone call, and a confirmation email from Rina. Like the Tazmanian Devil, she brilliantly spun into my life, romanced the crap outta me and sealed the deal.

The next thing I knew, I had a month to prep a 5-minute talk around the theme Body Beautiful.

Piece of cake, I thought. Speech writing was my speciality. And content on the body? Pfffft. You couldn't have given me an easier topic. I had spent 43 years in deep conversation with my meat suit.

I sat down a couple days later and whipped together a comedic monologue that Nia Vardalos herself would have been proud of, saved my Word document as My Big Fat Greek Body, and basically forgot about it.

The month flew by and three days before the Speaker Slam competition, I was sitting on my bed putting the finishing touches on a corporate talk. I decided to take a break and review my Speaker Slam speech.

It was a funny talk, yes. Laced with sarcasm and self-deprecation, I felt pretty confident I'd get a few chuckles –at least from my mom and cousin Mary who I had coerced into coming. "It'll be 30 people at a bar. Just come for a laugh," I said. As I mentioned, I had no idea what to expect.

When I read over my speech, I suddenly had what I can only describe as a hot flash. Now for those not privy, imagine opening a burning hot stove and sticking your head into it. Yeah, that.

A flood of heat hit my face, poured over my shoulders and down my arms. The energy was palpable. I took pause and waited for it to pass. It didn't.

Now if you aren't into things magical, mystical or spiritual, I invite you to skip this next page and save yourself the eye roll. Because, what happened can only be described as a Divinely timed pattern interrupt.

A pattern interrupt occurs when a particular thought or behaviour abruptly changes. It's a technique used in neurolinguistic programming and behavioural psychology to move someone out of habitual thought patterns. We can *intend* a pattern interrupt by making a conscious choice or decision. For example, I now *choose* to get up 15 minutes earlier every day to meditate. I now *choose* to stop snacking after dinner.

But that's not exactly what happened in my case. And this is why I call it Divinely timed. Something *bigger than me* instigated the pattern interrupt and rocked me out of my reverie.

Now, I am fully aware I may lose some of you here. But at least, this early in the game, you haven't invested too much of your valuable time and you can bail.

For the rest of you brave (perhaps only curious) souls, I'll share that I wholeheartedly believe that the 'hot flash', this pattern interrupt, and the pause it invited, was a clear pivot point on my path.

Now, I don't subscribe to the idea that we have a planned destiny or that our life story is predetermined in any way. What I do believe, is that we each have a soul contract for our lifetime. An agreement of sorts about what we intend to learn, how we will leave our imprint or expand our spiritual awareness. It doesn't really matter what you believe, but I think most of us would agree that there are moments in life that, looking back, forever change the course of our life path. And whether that is planned or intended, synchronistic or completely random, that's what happened to me.

I could easily have overridden the feeling and just stuck with my original speech. But I didn't. And for good reason. At this point in my life, I had already had countless opportunities to experience Divine intervention (also known as inner guidance, intuition, the Voice, Higher Self), and had learned, often painfully, the repercussions of ignoring it.

So back to my hot flash. It was uncomfortable enough to stop me in my tracks and make me pay attention and get curious.

I had a moment of reckoning with myself (don't freak out, this is very normal for me).

I said, "Self, you don't have time for this BS. You have a paying gig that you need to prep for right now. Let this go."

Awkward pause as Self waits for me to catch up with my Knowing.

Deep sigh. "Ok, Self, I see you're not going to let this go. Here's the deal. You have ONE hour to rewrite this speech. One hour, ya hear?"

And the Too Much Woman speech poured out of me like syrup on pancakes. (Oh, and get used to the food metaphors. I'm Greek and Italian. Food is life.)

I don't remember writing it or editing it or thinking too hard about it.

I wrote without attachment or intention. Which, by the way, is the opposite of what a speaker or speechwriter typically does. I wasn't focused on the audience. I wasn't concerned with outcomes or take-aways. I had no agenda or extrinsic motivation. I just wrote my truth. And as romantic as that sounds, I wasn't even trying to be poetic about it.

I asked myself the big, final question that I asked guests on my podcast interviews, *If the world fell silent and you held the only microphone in your hand, what would you really want to say?*

I think there was immense freedom in knowing that I had a back-up speech in case I chickened out. It also helped that no one in the audience would know me or have any expectation. And in that space of absolute detachment, I let the words run through me.

I sent an email to Rina, one of the hosts of Speaker Slam, to tell her I had rewritten my speech and ask that she hold me accountable for not regressing to my original stand-up routine.

It's fair to say, as soon as I wrote the words, they were precious to me, and I had some trepidation about sharing them. Like any creation birthed from pure curiosity, honesty and vulnerability, my writing was sacred. And sharing it felt like turning myself inside out.

Nobody knew anything about the experiences I described in my speech. For years I had tucked them carefully away in my Closet 'O Shame. I even convinced myself I was a strong person because I dealt with it all solo. The childhood abuse, the bullying, the sexual harassment at work. I had never told a soul. Ever. I also thought I was so 'over it' – I mean, I teach this stuff and surely I'd healed from all of that by now.

With total transparency, I really didn't think most people would even *get* the message of The Too Much Woman. Having worked with countless of women over the years, the consistent pain point was Not Enoughness. (Which is actually related, but we will discuss this in the next chapter.) And I didn't have the time in a 5-minute speech to connect all the dots.

So, essentially, I wrote the truth, I held my breath, I said the thing.

Then, I won the contest.

This would be a good story even if it ended there. It didn't. Little did I know this was only the beginning.

I woke up the next morning to a flood of social media messages from people who had been at the competition. Nearly 200 people attended Speaker Slam and I'm pretty sure every one of them and their momma reached out to me that next day. It was overwhelming to hear from so many that they related to dimming themselves down over the course of their lifetime.

I was surprised at the vulnerable shares from strangers, men and women alike.

Two days later, as a result of my win, Dan, one of the hosts of Speaker Slam, posted a video of my speech. I shared it on my Facebook business page to about 3000 followers and went to bed.

The next morning, I woke up to over 700 Facebook notifications and my video had tens of thousands of views. Too Much Woman was the earthquake that spurred the tsunami. The giant had awoken.

THE MAGIC

Over the next few months, the messages continued to flood my inbox, hundreds of them. Stories of shame and rejection, stories of abuse and regret, stories of defiance, rebellion and triumph. So many stories.

I spent hours reading and responding to each one. Everyone told me I was nuts! I felt accountable for acknowledging the brave souls who shared such intimate moments with a total stranger. I felt responsible for opening the Pandora's box of feelings and frustration about not feeling safe to show up as they were. I felt protective, like a momma bird, of their vulnerability, wanting to brew a vat of soothing hot chocolate with marshmallows so we could all sit cozily around a burning fire and be affirmed by our not-aloneness.

And then, just when I thought my heart would burst from so much love and hope and inspiration, Goalcast, an online media platform, shared my video, and blew the roof off of my life.

Within days, millions watched the Too Much Woman speech, then tens of millions.

I remember at one point, decidedly taking a 30-minute break from my phone to enjoy coffee with a friend, and returning to over 400 Facebook notifications alone! This happened all day long.

Facebook repeatedly put me in 'jail', blocking me from accessing my account due to suspicious spammy behaviour because of the thousands who joined my groups and my business page. Sitting behind bars, I continued to read the endless messages and comments with a mix of confusion and curiosity. Not only did I feel that my Too Much story was unique to me, but it didn't support the long-standing narrative that I observed on a daily basis among women.

See, I'm in this unique position where I encounter hundreds of amazing women through my work both as an international speaker and a social media blogger.

You know those women? Maybe you're one of them. They are kind, thoughtful and intelligent. They are great moms, wives, entrepreneurs, nurturers and healers. They are generous with their time and words, and always go above and beyond for people they care about. They have great ideas, they genuinely want to make a positive impact and they are ready to push up their sleeves to support something they deeply believe in.

My heart is so full for these brilliant women. Women who know, deep down, that there is something they were born to do. Some way they are meant to serve. Some space they alone are meant to fill.

And women who, for whatever reason, cannot always see their own brilliance.

Women who are convinced that their medicine needs more perfecting, more refining, more time to be alchemized before sharing it with the world.

Women playing small in life, in relationship and with their dreams because the sap of self-doubt has disabled their courage.

To explain this, many point to a widely accepted narrative, particularly for women, which has us steeped in a deficit of "Not Enough-ness."

I hear this all the time. *I'm not smart enough, I don't know enough, I'm not young/old/savvy/pretty/thin/sophisticated/confident enough.*

What I have come to discover, is that **a *parallel and opposing storyline that is not being discussed*** is running, that is just as destructive, and just as successful in keeping a woman small.

This is the untold story of the **Too Much Woman**.

Too intense. Too sensitive. Too emotional. Too passionate. Too driven. Too smart. Too sensual. Too needy. Too ambitious. Too fat. Too dramatic. Too honest. Too pretty. Too wild. Too successful. Too intimidating. Too sexy. Too rebellious. Too controlling.

The **Too Much Woman** is forced to cram the Bigness of who she is into a tight box of predictability and stability.

Her bright sparkle must be dimmed. Her radiance must be kept in check. Her energy on lockdown.

The Too Much Woman is not safe in a world that is afraid of her power. She is shunned, misunderstood, ignored, rejected, abused, threatened, objectified. Anything, anything, anything that will keep her tucked in her smallness and not threaten the status quo.

As women, many of us straddle these two debilitating paradigms: subduing our **Too Muchness** and ruminating in our **Not Enough-ness** –they are in fact opposite sides of the same coin, after all.

I am Too Sensitive, therefore not tough enough.

Too Dramatic, therefore not subdued enough.

Too Bold, therefore not timid enough.

Too Sensual, therefore not chaste enough.

Too Confident, therefore not humble enough.

Too Ambitious, therefore not Unassuming enough.

Too Intense, therefore not playful enough.

Too Passionate, therefore not placid enough.

Too Needy, therefore not secure enough.

Too Wild, therefore not tame enough.

Always forced to walk the tightrope, balancing the precise measurement of a woman, as though she is a recipe. An acceptable pinch of this, a predictable splash of that.

My personal story is about oscillating between radiating in my Too Muchness, and dimming in my belief of Not Enoughness, as a result of painful repercussions from shining too brightly.

I, like many women I have heard from, and even some men, have been abused, shunned, rejected, ignored, criticized and taken advantage of, for expressing all of myself. And as a consequence, I became very small, hiding from myself and my best life. When my daughter was born, I worried that she too, would be forced to pack her Too Muchness down into an acceptable size, in order to be loved and accepted in this world.

I am quick to emphasize that I will not further disempower myself by calling myself a victim. This doesn't mean paradigms and beliefs don't have to change, or that I don't support holding others accountable for their actions. What it means, for me, is perfectly described by Marianne Williamson in her book *A Woman's Worth*, when she says, "Womanhood is being recast, and we're pregnant, en masse, giving birth to our own redemption."

And so, on that crisp March night, in a club called Lula Lounge, I told the truth, bringing forth life in a way I never had before. And overnight, I heard the echoes of thousands of women around the globe who were gestating, and also ready to deliver themselves.

And the Too Much Woman Movement was born.

How I Got Here

I'm quick to defend that I'm not an overnight success or a flash in the pan. What many don't know about my journey as a professional speaker is that it began almost two and a half decades ago. I put my time in y'all! My viral videos (two at time of writing), are the result of years of honing my craft and developing my style, and of course, a huge splash of Divine Timing and Grace.

And just as I never intended a viral video, the birth of a movement or even a global tour, I also never planned on becoming a speaker. This is how it happened.

My professional career began when I freakishly landed a position in the newsroom at CityTV, a popular 24-hour news station in downtown Toronto. I had no journalism experience or industry connections. Just a freshly celebrated double honours degree in Media Communications and English, with a minor in Spanish, oh, and a horseshoe up my arse. I didn't know what I wanted to do with my life since I had let the dream of a career on Broadway die. I was ambitious and bright-eyed and ready to take on the world. I just didn't have any *specific* direction on how.

On a crisp October morning, I was headed downtown with my best friend Marty and her six month old son Calvin. She was on her maternity leave and was always coming up with new things for us to do together. CityTV was hosting their annual Open House and she suggested we head downtown to explore the newsroom and check out the sets of some the popular shows.

I was still living with my parents at the time and I remember joking with my mom while putting on my shoes to leave that day that I was going to get a job there. She responded with, "I don't have a doubt in my mind." We laughed and laughed. When we arrived at the news station, there was a line five people deep that wrapped around the entire building. Calvin was asleep in his stroller, so we passed the time catching up as best friends do.

About 20 minutes into our wait, I noticed one of the prominent news reporters Cynthia Mulligan working her way down the line with a camera man behind her. She was shooting a live broadcast interviewing random people about why they had come down to the Open House. I *willed* her to come to me. I remember staring at her and imagining her walking right up to me and shoving the mic in front my face. And then she did. Now, I love to say that it was my stealth Jedi powers that magnetized her to me, but with total transparency, Calvin had just woken up from his nap and was nestled adorably in my arms. He was a magnet.

The next thing I know, we are live. She asked the routine questions like why we were there and where we had come from, but all the magic happened after the segment was over and the camera was off. Cynthia and I exchanged some small talk, and then she asked me what my professional plans were. I told her I really wanted to follow in her footsteps. In fact, I may have said it was my dream to work as a journalist.

She smiled sweetly and said there was a year long waiting list, and suggested I just *volunteer* to answer the phones at the front desk of the newsroom, with the slim hope of getting a foot in the door. The competition was fierce and applicants numerous. She also said she couldn't do much to help, but she liked my spunk and gave me the number of one of the producers. I thanked her, called him immediately and landed a meeting.

The next thing I know, I'm hired.

At home we celebrated like had I won an Academy Award—special dinner, champagne, fine china…after all, I had *arrived*! This was beyond spectacular. My family was so proud!

So, four months in, when I drafted my letter of resignation and quit my job, I pretty much had to use smelling salts to revive my mother. If I am honest with myself, I can say I knew right away that journalism was not for me.

I'd been feeling like the Grim Reaper—gathering the worst news of the day and disseminating the dire state of the world upon the masses. Dramatic perhaps, but I definitely knew it was not the energy I wanted to put into the world.

I'd stuffed my disappointment and shame down deep. I was supposed to be happy. This was an opportunity of a lifetime. What was *wrong* with me? I started to feel so heavy. Exhausted. I slept all hours if I wasn't working, I was trying to escape the voice telling me this was a big mistake.

Every day I dragged my lead-filled legs to work, and I would sit in my car half paralyzed in the parking lot, *willing* myself to start my shift.

It wasn't long before the headaches began, then the throbbing pain in my neck. And when those weren't enough to get my attention, the Universe sent hives. My body was on fire with red splotches that no naturopath or allergist could diagnose.

I knew at a soul level what was happening. I embodied the stress of disappointing the producer Clint who had taken a huge chance on me, my mentor Mark Daily who generously invested so much personal time training me on set, my family who was over-the-moon about seeing me on TV, the whole entire world who would surely be devastated if I quit, and mostly myself. I agonized about letting myself down. And one day, as I sat miserably, for the gadzillionth time in the parking lot before my shift, I caught my red-rimmed eyes in the rear-view mirror and silently said, *enough*.

I honestly don't think my feet touched the ground as I flew out of the building after resigning that day. I felt light and free, and mostly so proud of how I had finally honoured myself. I sang the whole way home and felt more energetic than I had in months.

But that bubble burst soon after that. My well-intentioned friends and family told me I was nuts throwing away the opportunity of a lifetime. What did I *do*? This was a doorway that had opened for me and I was quitting too soon. As a lifelong people pleaser, I was tormented by everyone's opinions and lack of faith in my decision. I was also young and disillusioned about success and how to go about 'getting it', so I did the unthinkable.

I put my tail between my legs, drove to the newsroom and begged for my job back.

And unbelievably, unfortunately, I got it.

Then the real torment began, because I now had to prove I was worthy of a job I didn't even want! I probably *should* have won an Academy Award for my performance. I mustered up the façade of enthusiasm and dedication of a stellar young journalist. I worked on overdrive, through my days off, going in early and coming home late. I tried so hard to will myself to love it, to appreciate it, to make it work. I would prove to everyone I wasn't a quitter after all.

My redemption barely lasted a few months. I crashed hard. And hit an all-time low.

Back to the drawing board. It was humiliating and humbling.

Out of necessity, I got a job in the call centre of a collections department for a local telephone company, biding my time until I could figure out next steps. I accepted my Grim Reaper's karma and spent my summer in a two-by-two cubicle, tethered to a desk, reciting a script that ensured I maintained superior customer relations and a call length under 90 seconds. It was a brutal job.

About 6 months in, an opportunity opened up in the training department. The company, previously a monopoly, would now have to contend with competition. It was looking for trainers to deliver customer service courses. This was my ticket to get off of the front lines. What I didn't know was how perfectly the Universe had lined up this opportunity.

By day, I ran workshops for my peers. By night, I aggressively poured myself into personal development books. The lines started to blur and everything I was learning about empowerment started to show up in my classes. The positive feedback from my sessions caught the eye of my manager and few others. People gravitated to my classroom, rearranged their schedules so I could teach them and some even came back early from their vacation to fit into my training schedule.

I was happier than I had been in a long time. So enthused about life and motivated to grow. My friends noticed the change in me and asked me to share what I was learning. I synthesized some material and invited a group of friends to meet in my basement once a month. There was no fee. The exchange was a yummy potluck, meaningful conversation, oh, and a lightbulb. The lightbulb over my head lit up after my first session when I realized that by helping others find their power, I had found mine.

I initially registered my business with the sole purpose of honing my craft as a facilitator and optimistically breaking even. The meetings in my basement grew exponentially. "Can I bring my sister? My aunt needs to hear this!" I was forced to rent out spaces to manage the volume. Within a few months, through word of mouth, I was offered one thousand dollars to speak to a group of bank managers. It may well have been one million dollars. I prepared for that talk like my life depended on it. I thought it was the greatest blessing in the world, to speak to and inspire others. I still feel that way over 24 years later.

In less than a year, I was working regularly as a corporate trainer. Within two years, I was hired as an independent consultant by an international training company and was facilitating and speaking across industries and around the country on a regular basis. Things moved quickly. I was up-leveling my skills, my knowledge base and my self-concept exponentially. My journalistic roots served me well as I researched topics for talks and workshops. I poured myself into personal growth and I even got certified by the legendary Brian Tracey.

To this day, I continue to balance all the legs of my business.

I still travel globally to speak on leadership, service and communication in corporate spaces. I continue to host live events on subjects I am passionate about. I blog daily on Facebook and Instagram to an incredibly supportive, loyal and loving tribe. I host a podcast called Spiritual G Spot. I have recently launched an online platform for deeper self-awareness and spiritual growth. I am currently on the Too Much Woman Global Tour connecting with extraordinary women across the world. It is all very fulfilling, a bit overwhelming, and a smidge cray-cray. I mean, how is this my life? I could never have planned *this*.

But here's the dig.

I've never truly felt successful. For most of my career, rooted in me was this dark belief that I was an imposter, that what I was doing wasn't enough, that I wasn't thriving.

And this is what I want you to hear.

For so long, true success for me, meant unlimited affluence, employees to pay and an interview with Oprah Winfrey. Reading business books and attending seminars to *Boost Profits* and *Expand Your Customer Base* only illuminated the ways I wasn't growing fast enough building my empire. The outside voices kept asking, Shouldn't I be further along? How can I grow this thing? And why wasn't Oprah calling?

Of course, I was really looking for some external validation, a clear stamp of approval from the Universe that I was worthy. Gosh, it always does come back to that for me.

The entrepreneurial world can be a scary one, especially when blindly forging your own path.

So, I began researching success. What was it? How do I get it? What was I doing *wrong*?

I didn't ultimately find the answer in a book, on the internet, or by speaking to successful people. I found the answer by reviewing my life.

For me, success is a path lined with a set of flags, each bringing me closer to my personal entrepreneurial nirvana. The first flag of success meant quitting my soul-sucking job and trusting my gut. The second was breaking away from the secure corporate training world to craft a life where I could create my own schedule and also be autonomous with my content, so I could feel I was sharing something meaningful with the world.

Subsequent flags included a business plan that allowed me the financial freedom to start a family, be home to raise my children through their formative years and schedule my days around dentist appointments, yoga classes and school trips with my kids. Today, I have stretched my definition of success to include putting energy into the world that showcases my unique gifts, being abundantly rewarded for being of service, prioritizing pleasure, modeling joy for my children, time freedom, radiant health, world travel and using my platform to shine light on others' gifts and talents. And the path continues.

The very first step to success, business or otherwise,

is taking the time to thoughtfully define it *for yourself*,

based on what is important to *you*.

It takes time. It takes grit. It takes sincerity. It takes honesty and introspection. It takes a double dose of courage and triple scoop of faith. Mix it all together and we find our days filled with meaning and fuelled by a spectrum of success markers that are both attainable and rewarding. In this way, we are no longer striving for a finish line that continues to blur and elude us like a mirage in the desert. When my definition of success is clearly defined by *me*, I am empowered to decide day by day, if I'm on the right track.

Profits and growth are not the only yardsticks to measure the success of business. My personal yardsticks include how amazing I feel on Monday mornings while the rest of the world moans and groans, the spontaneity of a mid-day walk in nature, volunteering at my kids' school, the opportunity to stretch myself every day to create meaningful content, receiving a raving testimonial from a client or the privilege of speaking to a roomful of soul-seekers.

Woven into the fabric of the entrepreneurial mindset, is this toxic belief that bigger is better, profit is power and sales are supreme. I bought into this belief years ago, and I'm looking for a refund.

As a female entrepreneur in the 21st century, I stand for a radically new definition of success—one that encompasses all of the roles I play and financially honours the energy I put out into the world. It is my *responsibility* and my *privilege* to craft my personal definition of success. And it is yours.

"Today you are You, that is truer than true.

There is no one alive who is You-er than You." Dr. Seuss

I don't come from a family of entrepreneurs. My posse tends to shoot for the 25-year gold watch and fringe benefits. So, I have always been hungry for a mentor—someone to show me *the way,* to make it easy for me, basically to save me. I'm pretty sure this is called the Prince Charming Syndrome.

I always fantasized about an older female sage, cloaked in a white toga, infusing me with her knowledge and guiding me to make smart business decisions, while a harp plays softly in the background. When she didn't arrive, I latched onto the coattails of the first successful entrepreneur I could find. My guru took the form of a charismatic 29 year old businessman named Philip Murad.

Philip was a big thinker, a risk-taker, a marketing maverick and I admired the way his brain worked—probably because it was *so* different than mine. I watched him closely, taking mental notes as his business grew exponentially, thinking to myself, "I'll just replicate whatever he's doing." I slowly became aware of the great divide between his business approach, unique talents, and my own—realizing that I would have to forge my own path.

Over the years, I have met many entrepreneurs. I have read their books, participated in their seminars, and picked their brains. I have gained tremendous value in their wisdom, especially in areas that I know little about. I am a lover of learning, so more was always better –more opinions, more approaches, more guidance. The voices in my head got so loud I soon couldn't hear my own and often lost touch with the essence of *my* gift. And after years of trying to squeeze myself into their well-worn jeans, here is what I know for sure.

I *cannot* be successful by being anything but authentically me.

I am most impactful, most valuable to my audience, most energized, most profitable–when I am most 'Gina'. A mentor can show you *a* way, *their* way, to success, but it's only *their* way. Not the *only* way. We mustn't be afraid to blaze our own trails and off-road a little while doing so; trusting our inner GPS to bring us home to a place we recognize.

I have been paralyzed and intimidated by the thought of all the competition out there and all of the ways I must stay competitive in the game. While there may be many people doing *what* I do, there is no one doing it the *way* I do it. And the same is true for you. Never underestimate the value of your unique fingerprint on the world. And never doubt that there is audience hungry for what you're uniquely serving.

When the comparison monger starts to get to me, I reflect on a great idea I learned from Tara Mohr, in her book *Playing Big*. She suggests looking up book reviews for one of your favourite authors. Read some really positive ones and read some really negative ones too. See how diametrically opposed they are: "Her prose is so expressive and thoughtful! I couldn't put the book down!" and "Ugh, what a bunch of bologna! Her characters are two dimensional and un-relatable. Waste of time." This helps to get perspective on feedback and unique value. It emphasizes the importance of putting out work that is the truest reflection of me, not what people need to hear, or want to hear, but what feels true for me. I am not going to be everyone's cup of tea and I don't need to be. That's what makes the Universe so abundant. There is room for all of us, all voices, all flavours, all shades of uniqueness.

It brings home my favourite Georgia O'Keefe quote, "You can be the juiciest, ripest peach on the tree, and there will be somebody who doesn't like peaches." I am definitely not for everyone. And I am finally getting that that's pretty freaking okay.

Timing is *not* everything.

Oprah Winfrey was looking straight at me. Her mouth was moving and I'm pretty sure words were coming out. All I heard was Charlie Brown's teacher, "Wah wah wah". *Oprah Winfrey was talking to me!* She was answering a question I can't even remember asking. A question about timing. "How do you know when it's time to pursue your dream? When can you trust the time is *right*?"

It was definitely an out-of-body moment. I was at a taping of an Oprah Winfrey show called "What Do I Want to Do with My Life," showcasing entrepreneurs who successfully pursued their passions. Synchronicity was flaunting her impeccable sense of timing because, eight years into my speaking business, I was at a crossroads. On the one hand, I had an impossible dream that ached to be realized. I wanted to launch and grow an international show. On the other, I didn't have the experience, know-how or the audacity to believe I could make it happen.

The audience was thrilled to be gifted with free mink slippers and red velvet cupcakes, but I was tormented by the notion of timing. I didn't even hear Oprah's response to my question until I got home and reviewed the VHS tape that had recorded the episode.

"Perfect time? There's no such thing. *Now* is the time. Don't wait for the perfect moment—it will *never* come. If you feel a Divine spark to do something, if that call pulls you toward it, then baby, you'd better answer the call."

This would still be a great story if I told you that my life changed in that moment, that I mustered the faith and courage to chase my dream because 'Oprah said so'. Sorry to disappoint. It seemed I lost my confidence on the flight home from

Chicago to Toronto. And although I did *slowly, eventually* move in the direction of my big dream, it took me nearly a decade to really internalize what she meant.

There are a million reasons *not* to start now: the economy, personal finances, time restraints, familial responsibilities, lack of resources, discomfort, *sigh,* my thighs.

There is only one reason to start now: *Now is the only moment we have.* Ugh, I know it sounds so cliché, but stick with me a second.

I'm here bumping along on this journey called life just like you.

Truth is, sometimes I wake up with clarity and I nail it. Other days I wake up in a London fog and feel like I'm in Spiritual Kindergarten all over again. This is what the journey's all about.

On golden days it's melodic. Many days it's freaking noisy. And some days I don't even have words to describe it (just a whole bunch of obscene hand gestures). But I make a commitment to Show Up. Every damn day.

To ask better questions. To get curious about the answers. To practice my craft. To be accountable to all of you. To be resilient. To be human -vulnerable -powerful all in one breath.

That's the Who I choose to be.

Radical honesty is like a whore in stilettos sometimes. Not always pretty to look at and often uncomfortable to be around, and yet beautifully vulnerable, oddly tempting and not something you wanna mess with until you are good-and-ready.

So I'm here to light the way for you. To hold a safe space as you pull out your flashlight and dare to peek into those dark spaces.

You're going to feel a lot of ups and downs. (Normal)

And your armpits will get sweaty. (Again, normal)

It's part of the process. And you are not alone.

Be gentle with yourself, darling.

But promise me one thing.

No matter the score, stay in the game.Top of Form

When I get weak at the knees and my reptilian brain urges me to flee, I remind myself that I don't need to know the next 20 steps -only the next step. I dig deep -past the naysayers, the media, the critics, the well-meaning advice and finally, past my comfort zone into the deepest part of myself.

I get quiet and tune into my inner guidance that softly whispers, "Yes".

Although the road is not always straight or clear, I know that any step, even *small* ones, even *wrong* ones, move me forward. When the fear and doubt creep up, put your hand on your heart. That *thump, thump, thump* is the ticking hands of time, reminding you of its flight, which none can stop, and money cannot buy.

Now is the time. Start small. Start anywhere. But start.

And if you are waiting for a sign...*Baby, this is it*.

TOO DRAMATIC

There's a joke in my family that I took the song "*It's my party and I'll cry if I want too*" a little too seriously. Apparently, I cried at **every single one** of my birthday parties. Apparently, there are even pictures to prove it. Apparently, it's a no-win argument for me.

Exhibit A-Z: Pictures of me posed behind my annual birthday cake with the sequential numeric candle stuck deep in the chocolate frosting announcing my new age...3, 6, 9.

My eyes, a deep pool of Mediterranean green-blue, freshly sparkling from the tears. Face splotched with pink puddles of emotion. Feigning a smile because my mother had shot me The Look and I had *better get-with-the-program* because this was a magical moment dammit, and she was about to take a picture to prove it.

I honestly don't remember why I cried.

Maybe my party dress was itchy. Maybe I hated my ridiculous bowl-cut. Maybe the cake was the wrong flavour. Maybe I was overwhelmed by all the noise and fuss.

Maybe I felt the energy of all the adults in the room who wanted me to hurry-the-fuck-up-so-they-could-go-the-hell-home already.

Maybe I could sense the tension, the sadness, the worry, the exhaustion all crammed into our family room where we had Big Fat Greek parties with a gazillion people, crying babies, cranky kids, loud talking aunts, louder talking uncles, fake smiles, big personalities, unfulfilled dreams, untold stories and married people who secretly hated one another.

Maybe I just needed a nap.

Hell, maybe I *was* a Drama Queen.

The name stuck to me like sap and with it, the sticky inner belief that my feelings weren't valid or important or real. They were abnormal, ridiculous and attention seeking.

Ultimately, I swallowed my emotions. Gobs of them. Choking them down like cotton balls.

My drama scraping the neck of my throat on its way down. Resisting like a kid on a too big slide-clutching the sides with all limbs -desperate to get back up and out.

No wonder the chronic sore throats All My Life. No wonder the incessant coughs.

So much swallowing. And gagging. And swallowing again.

The irony is that I speak for a living.

Talking. Telling. Sharing. Outpouring. Confessing. Claiming. Naming.

And I am paid for it. Ha. Maybe this is winning.

I think this is why I was so drawn to the arts. Dancing and acting gave me a safe space to feel, a place where my emotional expression was acceptable, even celebrated. In the tenth grade, I auditioned for the annual school play *The Glass*

Menagerie by Tennessee Williams. There were only four parts in the play: two female and two male. I was desperate to get one of the two coveted female roles. I went to an all-girls Catholic high school and our plays were done in collaboration with the all-boys school up the road. So, competing with an entire high school for one of two roles, my chances were slim.

I think I was the only one who read the play twice as preparation for the try out, and then watched the movie. (I had a creative crush on John Malkovich). I remember being heartbroken for the main character Tom. He worked in a shoe factory by day, doing his best to support his mother Amanda, a faded Southern belle, and his physically and emotionally crippled sister Laura. He was tethered to his miserable life by this obligation, while he longed to write poetry and escape to travel the world.

What part of me, as a young girl at age 15, could relate to this character? I cannot say. But it *gutted* me. I cried big fat alligator tears alone in my room for Tom. Something about his desperation moved through me with an echo of resonance – perhaps a recollection from a past life? Or more absurdly, the prediction of a future experience? All I know is, when I went to read for the parts of Amanda and Laura, all I could think about was Tom.

You can imagine my shock when Mr. Lavery, the play's director, pulled me aside in the hallway the day after the audition, to ask me if I was willing to cut off all my hair for Tom's role. It was a *'Hell yes!'* without a second thought. Oh, he added, and would I be willing to learn to smoke a cigarette?

The experience of preparing for that role, was pivotal in my Too Dramatic story. Mr. Lavery, God bless that man, spent hours with me, like pizza dough, kneading, working in and smoothing out the dramatic nuances the character demanded to help me connect with and harness my creative expression. I credit him with holding space for me to safely explore all the forbidden corners of my dramatic curiosity. There was no shame, no tsk-tsking, no *look*, no eye roll, no reprimand. I was allowed, no, I was *celebrated*, for feeling, for crying, for exaggerating and for displaying my emotional range.

My Too Much Drama made him jump up and down with excitement, it made him clap his hands with affirmation, and on the evening of the performance, it even made him cry. I hold sacred in my heart the snapshot of a moment when he stood before me, behind the closed curtain as the audience cheered, holding my shoulders firm in his hands, tears in his eyes and said, "Thank You Tom." It was the anointing, the blessing, the healing, the salve that the little drama queen in me needed.

Tears chase each other down my cheeks as I reflect on this almost 30 years later. How unknowingly a soul can shift our self-perception and forevermore change the lens we use to look within? Wherever you are dear soul, I thank you.

TOO SENSITIVE

At the age of about 9, and for the duration of a year, I had relentless dreams of our home catching fire. Night after night I woke up shaking, sweating and screaming. My poor mom and stepdad did all they could to reassure me that we were safe and that a fire was highly unlikely. They weren't smokers, after all, and they were very careful when cooking. What started off as loving concern, evolved over time into weathered frustration. *"Gina, enough already!"*

At one point in desperation, my stepfather picked me up from a corner where I was hiding, and held me firmly beside the roaring fireplace in our family room to prove to me that I was safe while I shook, flailed and cried like a captive, wild animal.

In September of 1985, we moved into a new home and I urged my stepfather to test the smoke detectors on each floor of our split level. The one in the hall outside of the bedrooms was dead. *I freaked out.* He said it was probably the battery and he would replace it, not to worry. But I worried. Boy, did I worry.

My dreams became lucid and more petrifying. Every night, the same story. Me screaming "There's a fire–get out!" as my family sat calmly, playing cards around the kitchen table, ignoring my outbursts and shooting one another knowing looks about me, the crazy Too Sensitive child.

Celebrating the TOO MUCH WOMAN

That Christmas, with some holiday money from my grandfather, I walked to the local Home Hardware store and bought my family a brand-new smoke detector. I was adamant it be installed as soon as possible, and my stepfather acquiesced, to shut me up.

Two weeks later in early January, I awoke to the sounds of my family frantically running around the house, my mother's panicked voice on the phone sharing our address with a 911 operator, and her calling out to my stepfather, "Don't forget my fur coat in the front hall!"

Not another dream! I moaned. I pulled the sheets tightly around my head, attempting to drown out the sounds and the fury in my head. *What is wrong with me?* And then I heard it. First distant, then louder, and soon, impossible to ignore. Sirens, lots of them, bellowing urgently from the road. I jumped out of bed and peeked through the vinyl blinds out my window. It took me a moment to register what I was seeing. Not one, but five fire trucks lined the street, lights blaring as desperately as their wailing alarms.

My bedroom door opened. "Gina, we need to get out of the house–now."

I honestly don't remember what happened after that. I'm sure an accomplished psychotherapist could draw it out of the locked vault in my mind's eye, but I'm really not that interested. What matters is, we all made it safety out of the home and I later learned that my recently purchased smoke detector was the *only one* in the entire house that went off that night to save us when our furnace overheated.

That was a clue, in a sea of many, that my Too Much Sensitivity was not to be ignored.

Now, I don't think for a minute that I'm unique in this. After much research, I understand how we are all wired for sensitivity as a species. It was extremely validating, however, to learn that I fell into the twenty percent of the population called Highly Sensitive. I read a book by the same name in my 30's, written by Dr. Elaine Aron, and let out a sigh of relief I didn't know I was holding. Tears of self-recognition refreshed my perspective.

Okay, I'm not a freak, this is a thing, and maybe my sensitivity is a blessing rather than a handicap.

The pendulum started to swing *away* from seeing my sensitivity as something that I had to fix and override, and *towards* a new freedom where I could look with curiosity at how it could be my super power.

I started to connect the dots about how it has come to serve me in many ways. It has steered me clear of soul-sucking jobs, redirected me away from unhealthy relationships and situations, and shaken me out of my logical mind to see more clearly what wasn't so apparent to my unwilling eyes.

Most of all, my sensitivity has forced me to dig deep into myself, drilling down past layers of easy answers and habitual thought patterns, through shame and avoidance, toward pain and discomfort, into hard questions and honest answers and settling finally into vulnerability and acceptance.

I have come to learn that the more curious about and open to my sensitivity I become, the stronger its communication. I can meet someone and instantly detect their energy and level of sincerity. I can walk into a space and immediately pick up on the pulse in the room. When tapped in, my Spidey-senses can intuit roadblocks or potential problems before they arise, simply because I am tuned into a frequency that communicates using all of my senses, including my Inner Knowing.

I became so fascinated by this powerful level of discernment, I tapped into my journalistic roots and researched all I could find on the subject and ended up teaching workshops on it. I watched with fascination how my sensitivity was the gateway to greater compassion, deeper connection and unbound creativity.

Then I met Gabrial, a spiritual way-shower, who took me even deeper into understanding my gift and how to communicate more clearly with my Guidance using energy techniques. This upgraded my toolbox and I now use these on a daily basis to harness my sensitivity and gain clarity from my Inner Knowing.

There is no question my Too Much Sensitivity needs to be managed so I don't get overwhelmed, burnt out or over anxious. I have mastered ways to protect my sensitivity. For example, reducing the number of stimuli in my environment (bright lights, loud sounds, coarse fabric, violent movies), noticing early signs of overwhelm and agitation (limited large and noisy social events), plenty of alone time to process feelings and self-reflect (self-care practices such as journaling, epsom salt baths and nature walks).

Developing a 'thick skin' has never been my desire. I would rather feel the rub of every intense feeling than walk through the world detached, disconnected and unscathed.

My choice. My power.

And, P.S., for my own peace of mind, please check your smoke detectors.

TOO PROVOCATIVE

Dancing was my first passion.

Music was always playing in my childhood home. Mostly Motown and R&B, some Rock and Roll, a little Jazz, Greek classic folk songs, and endless Pop. I mean *always* playing.

I recently reconnected with a childhood friend who lived in my neighbourhood and one of the first things she said was, "I remember your mom was always blasting music and we could hear it outside while we played hide 'n' go seek."

And we danced! We laid down the boogie, we salsa'd, we tangoed, we did the hustle, and the moonwalk, and we jammed while my Uncle Nick played a mean air guitar solo standing on the couch, Springsteen blasting in the background. I don't think there is ever a time that we didn't dance.

We had a large living room space with a record player and two giant floor speakers. I spent 90% of my childhood putting on dance performances for my stuffed animals and imaginary friends on the chairs and couches that lined that room. I tell 'ya, Olivia Newton John, Michael Jackson, Bob Segar, Stevie Wonder and The Pointer Sisters all performed to sold-out shows during the late 70's and early 80's on 121 Silas Hill Drive.

I started formal dance classes when I was three. Jazz, tap, ballet, break dancing (remember k-way pants?), anything that was available on a single parent's income. My dance teacher, Miss Ginger, God I adored that woman, gave me every opportunity to shine on stage and she was a very special part of my childhood. I have fond memories of her hand stitching multi-coloured sequins to a plain leotard to cut costume costs for my mom and agreeing to let me dance every one of my jazz solos to a Prince song.

I stopped formal dance classes once I started university, swallowing the bitter pill that I would never make it as a professional dancer, and then naturally segued into night clubs. Something definitely shifted going from dance class to dance floor.

It was the eyes. How they watched me. How I liked it.

Performing *for* another - to gain their affection, attention, admiration, was a trap that I quickly fell into. It came from years of being praised and adored for my how I looked as a child and young woman. *Ahh, so this must be love.* And also, from years of being unseen by the father whose attention I craved. *Please see me!* (Insert ferocious jumping jacks here).

So I performed, like a circus monkey for the crowd, in all areas of my life, not just the dance floor. I never stepped off the stage, really. I was perpetually 'on'. No wonder the utter exhaustion. No wonder the chronic fatigue. No wonder the insatiable tapeworm in my soul so hungry to be *seen*.

Dancing in night clubs became my heroin. A self-professed Good Girl all my life -the straight-A student, the helper, the nurturer, the responsible one, the prude, the valedictorian, I found that in my early twenties, I was hungry. Starved for fun and rebellion, ravenous to unlock hidden parts of myself I had locked in a chastity belt of judgment.

In dance-clubs, under the smoky haze of cigarette smoke and dizzying strobe lights, I could safely explore the buffet of my desires: my sensuality, my body, my eroticism. I didn't have to compromise myself either. I could just move my body, and revel in the heat and lust that hung in the air around me. That was as risqué as I would get. Walk into club, get the hit, drive home with my girlfriends. I was the quintessential cock tease: flirtatious and seductive on the dance floor, modest and cool off of it.

I longed for male intimacy, I craved love and attention and was also deeply distrustful of men. I hung out in the space in between. Nipping the bud of my hunger, without ever feeling full. Kind of like being on a green juice diet: you may fill the belly, but it's just not going to give you the emotional satisfaction that tacos can. (Remember, food is life.)

At some point, the game stopped being fun. I had always been a spiritual seeker and could no longer ignore that fact that I had come to a dead end on this road. Although the attention was tantalizing, and it was, it wasn't bringing me any closer to what I wanted. What I clearly wanted was validation wrapped in a security blanket of safety.

My subconscious was trained to seek worthiness from another's gaze, another's love, another's affirmation. I wanted to feel safe in that space. I craved a place I could curl into (like, oh, say, a man's arms), that would anchor me in my worth. I was the poster child for a girl with Daddy Issues, *and I knew it*.

So I stopped dancing and clubbing. I just cut it out of my life completely. And I started focusing on filling the void in other, more productive, more conscious, more 'spiritual' ways. I made a list of *Things I Wanted in a Partner* on a green notepad, sitting poolside on a business trip to L.A. I still have that list.

I thought I was so brilliant and intentional in my clarity. *Look at you*, I said to myself smugly, *being all conscious and stuff!*

I thought I was super self-aware to notice that I was seeking my father's love in all the wrong places, and that, instead, I would fill that need with a caring, trustworthy, dependable man. I was proud to have overridden my unconscious behaviour with a positive, healthy intention. So, I started dating a wonderful man who absolutely adored me. I have always said you could put him in a room full of naked women and I could trust his devotion. I settled comfortably into married life. I embraced nesting and domesticity. I birthed two spectacular children and threw myself into mothering like a champion. I sat on the parent committee at the kid's school, managed the pizza lunch and was on the bus at every class excursion. My kids and I went for long walks in the forest, stopping to follow meandering ants and pick wild flowers that we would later identify in books at the local library. We sang songs and played musical instruments, hosted pretend cooking shows and volunteered at local charities. I threw grand, themed birthday parties that took months to prepare for -simulating the Olympic games, an underwater expedition, a magic extravaganza, and a hoe-down complete with pony rides. Yup, I intended to earn that gold medal in the mothering department. I grew my corporate speaking repertoire and built a solid professional reputation for my communication expertise. I organized a free inspirational women's event in my home *every month for six years*. I got serious, very serious, some might say ridiculously obsessive, about getting fit and healthy. I bought organic-only food, I detoxed, I cleansed, I booty-camped and I swear I almost died on a 3-day juicing retreat. I scrubbed the house with a toothbrush, painted walls and wall-papered bathrooms. I meditated with Deepak Chopra, pumped my fist with Tony Robbins and spent thousands of dollars and hours on workshops, books and live speakers' series. I eventually hosted an online show called *Ignite a Life You Love* with a reach of over 70 countries globally, speaking with some of the most extraordinary people I could find. And somehow, this gal was deeply unhappy.

See, *every area of my life was lit up, except for one. The fire within myself.*

I looked to fill that original longing in all the places I could point to *out there*.

And when I took my finger and carefully traced it back to the starting line, I saw that it coincided with the time I stopped dancing. Like some kind of unconscious punishment, a jail sentence locking up my joy and sensuality, I obeyed the unspoken rule that a spiritual seeker, a professional, a wife, a mother, a woman of certain age didn't dare move her body like *that*.

I gave birth to my daughter at 31, and from her early days there was no doubt that dancing was in her blood. From the moment she could barely balance on her two wobbly legs and stand herself up against the couch, she would bop endlessly to the beat of the music. She flourished in her passion. Watching my daughter dance on stage stirred a longing in me to move my body again. To respond to a rhythmic beat of my spirit's music that only I could hear. And so, I did.

It felt very awkward in the beginning. Like young lovers experimenting with love making for the first time. My body, hot and bothered and full of desire, confused by tangled arms and legs out of rhythmic accord. I felt like a supreme dork, heavy and stiff, my head full of judgment, my sensuality tucked away somewhere in the attic of my soul alongside my university degree, my marriage, the birth of my two children, my role on the parent committee, my professional speaking career, cleaning toilets and last night's dirty dishes.

It took a while to come back to my body. To trust that it knew what to do. To give it permission to express itself without conforming to popular dance moves or frames in my mind's eye about the way I needed to look.

I'd like to say it was like riding a bike. I'd like to tell you that after some time, my muscle memory kicked in and I naturally adopted the suave and confident fluidity of my youth.

But I didn't. Something else happened.

Dancing actually made me sad.

I noticed how separate I was from myself. How disconnected I was from my Life Force. How in-my-head I has been living. How much I was operating from my masculine energy.

For all the spiritual work I had done on myself, and all the sessions I had taught my students, I still played by a handbook written in someone else's penmanship.

I was still seeking validation from outside of me.

And it had to stop.

There's a popular quote that dares us to 'Dance like nobody's watching'. There's freedom in dancing this way -unhinged and unobserved, unchained and unrestrained. There is deliverance in becoming untethered from the eyes of the Other. To move for the pure glory that movement can bring -the awakening of senses, the connection to Life Force, the embodiment of aliveness.

I started to dance around my kitchen when I was cooking, in my bedroom after a bath when I was feeling particularly sensual, with intention when I was down-and-out and wanted to change my vibration. I'd throw on a little Sade, a little Etta

James, a little Gloria Estefan, a little Beyonce, and just let myself go.

I danced, sometimes to express and move feelings *through* me (the good, the bad and the ugly), and other times to call energy *in*, or to summon a change or shift that my spirit required. I pulled out my old belly dance costumes and dared myself to not only try them on, but to dance in front of a full length mirror until I had shimmied off all of the critical voices that insisted I was being ridiculous.

I started salsa classes, tango, flamenco, bachata...with each slow, smooth turn, each rhythmic rise and fall of my chest, every intentional roll of my hips, I deepened my connection to myself. *Oh, hello gorgeous, where have you been all my life?*

It's no coincidence that at that exact time, the book *Pussy* was published, written by Regena Thomashauer. The book both mortified and intrigued me. For as much self-awareness and intentional work I had done on myself, I was bewildered by my body, my sexuality, my carnal desires. She literally and figuratively turned me on to the source of my feminine power which she describes as "the part of a woman [she has] been taught to ignore, push down and despise."

That book invited me to accept and declare for myself that *I am a sexual being!* There, I said it.

We have all been subconsciously conditioned to believe our innate sexuality is shameful, disgusting and wrong. This toxic belief has both women and men rejecting a core part of who we are, negatively impacting our emotional, physical and mental health.

The book propelled me to visit her for a Weekend Experience in NYC to explore my turn on and reconnect with that lost part of myself. That two-day event is difficult to describe. It wasn't at all about sex and orgasmic pleasure. It was an immersive experience that invited me to access my true power, beauty and brilliance. To reclaim my body's ways of communicating with me, guiding me and ultimately igniting the fire that had dimmed. To investigate what brought me pleasure and to follow those clues as the breadcrumbs that would lead me home.

Soon after that, I booked a boudoir shoot -something I kept in the drawer labeled "one day when…", more curious than anything about who exactly would dare to show up and pose in front of the camera at 40-something years old.

I started to feel alive, like a bear fresh from a long winter's nap, eyes blinking hesitantly at the brightness around me. Seeing anew my world, my power and most of all, myself.

My clothes changed, my stride changed, my energy changed, my writing changed. I felt fully alive and juicy, renewed and rebirthed.

And I began to magnetize my desires: people, opportunities, business. I just *turned on*, and allowed it to come to me, like bees to honey. This is how powerful self-ignition can be. It's wild, it's powerful, it's liberating, and if someone is not in their power, it's provocative indeed. See, provocation is less about me, and more about how someone receives my energy. It's hard to provoke anyone who chooses to remain detached, or who takes responsibility for their own feelings. I will end with a viewer comment and my response from my Facebook page on being too provocative.

November 15, 2018

Excerpt from a Private Message from "Natalie":

"I love your work," she starts, *"But why do you post pictures of yourself? Do you think maybe it turns the rest of us off? Makes*

us uncomfortable? I'm almost 70 and I love your exuberance, but maybe tone it down a bit? Maybe seeing you in a gorgeous pose takes away from other people's dreams for themselves."

My public response:

I love this woman. I really, really do.
Thank you N for your message.

You represent EVERY DARK DEMON hanging in my EGOIC CLOSET of SHAME.

You mark the PIVOT POINT on my laborious path of personal growth.

Like an x-ray, you radiate the fear and humiliation I embodied as a child that had me suffer the ignominy of my Too Much Body and the attention it garnered.

Lying in bed, reading your message, caused me to sit up and salivate at the opportunity to share my newfound personal freedom once again.

I've sung this song a hundred times, and I will repeat it until my mouth is parched and dry, until my last choked breath, until it echoes, shakes, reverberates and impregnates the womb of every hardened, shamed, and disgraced heart.

I will *not* dim any longer.

I have spent a lifetime, perhaps many, subduing my light, muting the glory of me, suppressing my fullness, burying my essence, camouflaging my Truth.

Like the sun, eclipsed by the moon, I too have let shame and doubt obscure my illumination.

Celebrating the TOO MUCH WOMAN

At 43, I am choosing to shine in all the ways.
With grace and dignity, with deep reverence and much discomfort, with pride and indignation, with absolute resolve and commitment.

I will shine like the freaking sun without apology.

My Too Muchness goes beyond my body.
It is the ENERGY of me, all I am that is God-given, my gifts, my awareness, my intention, my passion, my intellect.

If I dim in one area, I am disrespecting ALL.
If I hide one part, I throw shade on the others.

This is me.

I will not cover my mouth when I laugh too loudly.
I will not dull my joy when the world moans with fear.
I will not bind my breasts when I want to dance freely.
I will not ask for permission when I speak my truth.
I will not dumb down my words when I have something brilliant to say.
I will not smile prettily when I want to scream and cry.
I will not obey when I need to rebel.
I will not conform when my spirit feels threatened.
I will not succumb when I must defend.
I will not hide when rejection taunts me.

I will shine.
I will shine.
I will shine.

And I will celebrate you, my dear, when you are ready to shine too.

Gina

TOO VOLUPTUOUS

> "My truth, my words, my hips, my curves, two handfuls, maybe three…"

This is a great place to clear up some misconceptions about my message.

The Too Much Woman speech was written for a speaking competition where the theme was Body Beautiful. Yes, it was, in part, a defiant proclamation to own all parts of my curvaceous self, to reclaim my body from the critical gaze of the ever-observer, and release the shame associated with owning my sexuality, embracing my femininity, as well as celebrating my multiple handfuls.

I am a voluptuous woman. I jiggle when I walk, I need to buy specially made, over-priced bras to support my girls, and I have hips to make Shakira envious.

Some have come to my work mistakenly believing that the core message of the Too Much Woman is positive body image. And while I'm not here to define the meaning for anyone else, the message as intended by me, encompasses *the range of Too Much energy a woman holds: body, mind and spirit.* Bottom line, this isn't about me putting a stake in the ground for us Big Girls. This is way broader than the width of my hips.

Now, your access point into the Too Much Movement is yours to claim. And I honour that. Yay you! My passion, however, is way more expansive than a conversation around my body. With all due respect, that topic gets old -fast.

Firstly, my body is not my supreme offering to the world. It actually nauseates me to think of all the time I've spent obsessing, perfecting, dishonouring and even justifying it. I cringe to think that the masterpiece that is my creative gift to the world, all that I am, all that I share, all that I care deeply about, all that I labour over, all that I so lovingly craft to present to the world, can be swallowed whole in a mouthful composed of breast, thigh and ass.

Second, my body is not up for public debate. If I want to eat ice cream for breakfast, go Keto, become a vegan, or suck mashed potatoes through a straw, that's my business. Same goes for how I move my body, what I decide to pierce and what I choose wear. I have wasted a good chunk of my precious earthly visit standing in my closet wondering what *other* people would think looks good on me.

At 43 years old, I have never been more voluptuous. My curves have curves, baby. And interestingly, ironically, I have also never felt sexier, more alive, more confident, more rooted, more myself and more comfortable with my appearance. I'm not a narcissist. I'm not an egomaniac. And no doubt I'd love to improve some things here and there, but I have shifted into *ownership of my body*. A reclamation of its beauty, its power, its sovereignty, its sensuality, its right to feel feminine, sexy, powerful, strong, at this or *any* age, at this or *any* size.

It's mine. Full stop.

And I am grateful for it. How it's honoured me, forgiven me, blessed me, healed me, carried me, expressed me, protected me and stuck with me,

I mentioned earlier that I had boudoir-ish photo shoot. I say "ish" because it wasn't full on semi-nude lingerie style. I chose to wear things I felt sexy and powerful wearing.

This experience was a test for me, to see how it would feel to be seen in my Too Much Body.

When I was offered the opportunity to do a photo shoot, my gut clenched, and it was an immediate "*Hell no! I need some time to get my body in shape first!*" and that was the precise moment I knew I needed to do it.

This experience really wasn't about the pictures themselves -I actually didn't even get any printed. It was about that awkward moment between me and the camera. About the tension in the air when we first met eye to lens, and about the voices that carried on in my head, as I nervously offered up my body to be seen.

It was like putting a stethoscope against my awareness and daring to ask the question, *Why have I been given **this** body and what is it here to teach me?*

Although this is probably a question that I'll continue to ask until the moment of my death, I know it's an important one. I understand that this body has a bigger message for me about Reverence. Daring me to accept it *As Is*. To be comfortable with it, to befriend it, to celebrate it, to glorify it, to adorn it, to pleasure it, to dare to dance in it and be seen in its *full-on freaking glory.*

When I choose to be in this space of awareness, the power that erupts in me is *bigger than my breasts and more powerful than my thighs.* It makes me feel stronger than pumping iron and more invincible than skinny jeans ever will. I'm a Too Much Woman. And I'm not sucking it in any longer.

And to quote Forrest Gump, *That's all I have to say about that.*

TOO COMPLICATED

My family always jokingly said, *"Good luck to whomever gets her,"* and we'd laugh and laugh.

But damn, there's a grain of truth in all humour, isn't there? Good luck indeed.

No, I'm not an order-off-the-shelf kind of gal. I'm a mixed bag, an unexpected twist in the road, the surprise in your Cracker Jacks box, the lightning bolt from out of nowhere that scribbles its signature across the sky, the unexpected tidal wave that sucks you under, the extra shot of tequila that pushes you over the edge, the magic trick that makes you gasp with wonder, the luscious strawberry that bursts in your mouth, the rainstorm you can't decide whether to hide from or dance in, the last scoop of a hot fudge sundae you scrape off the bottom of the bowl even though you're about to burst –simply because you can't *not*.

I won't contort who I am to fit in the palm of anyone's expectations. No, not anymore. And, believe me, I'm not trying to be a badass about it. It is a very lucid and honest declaration.

I'm an acquired taste. My ingredients are on the label. Read them and decide for yourself. As Carrie Bradshaw declared,

Celebrating the TOO MUCH WOMAN

"I'd rather be someone's shot of whiskey than everyone's cup of tea."

It took me a long time to get here. I've traveled far and wide across the rocky terrain of my self-worth to arrive in a place where I honour the energy of me. I won't sit prettily wrapped in a savvy marketing package to win any buyer over. My spirit is not for sale.

I'm a wild one, a misfit, an emotional hurricane, a walking contradiction.

I am both Wild and Holy

Vulnerable and Guarded

Responsible and Reckless

Daring and Cautious

Courageous and Cowardly

Compassionate and Tough

Sexy and Homely

Ambitious and Lazy

Independent and Needy

Joyful and Melancholy

Popular and Lonely

Bold and Shy

Introverted and Extroverted

Complicated and Simple

I'm all this and a bag of chips. There's nothing wrong with me, and there's nothing wrong with you. I'm a beautifully complex, unabashedly multi-dimensional and proudly Too Much Woman.

And as I reclaim all the pieces of my Gina-self, I honour every rub and bump, every rip and tear that has etched itself onto the rock of my Soul.

This is me. Hot diggity damn, I think I love her.

Calling a woman high maintenance, too much work or too intense, overly *this* or too much *that*, is a great way to discredit the passion, effort and intention she puts into her life. It's certainly one way to dismiss her voice and her power.

A Too Much Woman is not to be tamed. She is to be adored, revered, celebrated, supported and seen. Her spirit needs to be free -given space to roam wild, explore the width and depth of her soul. And also grounded -anchored in truth and held in love.

Yup. Both.

And it won't take a saint or a martyr to love her. Just a soul who relishes in watching her flourish; someone ready to stand mountain to mountain with her power, anyone who understands that she will generously reciprocate in all the ways.

Baby, she's worth the effort. And yes, it takes a brave soul to love a woman like that.

TOO BOLD

"Watch out. She's a wild one. Always stomping on eggshells that everyone else tiptoed around." –K. Foster

In my first year of university, I took a class called Media Impact. It looked at multiple studies demonstrating the negative impact of television on behaviour, mood, intelligence and self-perception. (Ok, let me take you way back to a time before social media, iPhones and iPads. All we had was the TV, and we thought we had problems!)

Our final report was on a topic of our choosing and accounted for 40% of our final grade. I was a keen student. I knew what the professor wanted to hear and how to present a convincing argument. It was a no brainer for me, and I felt fairly confident I could ace it. I also felt compelled to ride the edge, to instigate, to challenge the status quo.

The essay I submitted was entitled, *"Everything I Needed to Know I Learned from Television"*. It was a complete contradiction to everything we were taught that year. It was rebellious, it was daring, and it earned me an A+.

In the twelfth grade, attending an all-girls Catholic high school, I presented a project in my religion studies class comparing many of the prominent religions and demonstrating how they were man-made mythologies. A stellar grade, and, oh, my teacher was a nun. Thank you, Sister Theresa.

Now, I wasn't always rewarded for taking risks. Many of my teachers appreciated my enthusiasm and how I spurred discussion in the classroom, and some had no idea what to do with my hutzpah. I wasn't your traditional trouble maker or attention seeker, you see. I was a straight A student, and hardworking, respectful, responsible and sincere.

I spoke up when I felt it was warranted, or to defend someone who didn't speak up for themselves. If I am anything, it's a ferocious protector and advocate for those who are taken advantage of, harmed or abused.

In the first grade, our teacher Mrs. Foy had a box of prizes hidden under her desk that she would award to children who were quiet. Midway through the year, a new little girl transferred to our school. English wasn't her first language and she undoubtedly felt overwhelmed. She spent the entire first week sobbing silently into her hands. The teacher, in complete frustration no doubt, announced that the little girl would not be getting a prize because she was acting like a baby. At recess, I snuck into the treasure box, stole a Minnie Mouse pencil set and defiantly laid it right on top of the little girl's desk. When Mrs. Foy asked who was responsible, I proudly stood up, looked my teacher in the eye and said "She deserves a prize! Even though she cried all week, *she didn't make a sound*! Fair is fair!" I was six.

Nothing much has changed over the years. I could fill pages with all the ways I broke trend, went against the grain, loudly advocated for social justice and dared to scribble outside the lines of convention in my life.

To be sure, my boldness wasn't always noble.

At thirteen years old, I walked into my bathroom with waist long hair and a pair of scissors, and walked out with a wild, uneven, Linda Evangelista-inspired pixie cut.

My boldness wasn't always smart.

I was once kidnapped by a public bus driver. I had stayed late at school practicing a monologue for a play and was catching the late bus home on a quiet street. It was a dark and cold winter's night and I was freezing. I didn't pay attention to the Out of Service sign on the bus that slowed to a stop in front of me and opened its doors. I scrambled on, eager to get warm, and immediately knew something was off. There wasn't another soul on the bus, the lights were dim, and the bus driver had a creepy look on his face. I quickly walked to back of the bus and rang the bell to get off. He kept just driving. Fast. Then faster. I yelled, *"Hey, I'd like to get off, you know!"* And he just started laughing. I started to scream and yell louder, and he just kept driving and laughing. I stopped screaming and centered myself. I got very clear about what I needed to do. I walked right up beside him. Looked him square in the face and said very firmly, *"Listen, you crazy bastard. Let me the fuck off of the bus, or I will report your sick ass."* He suddenly slammed on the brakes in the middle of the road, and luckily, I jumped out unscathed.

My intrepid behaviour has shown up in a boardroom confronting a patronizing CEO, in a hospital room with an insolent medical specialist and in my own bedroom during a sexual assault. I am forever grateful for the ways my Too Bold personae has caught air to ride up and out of my trembling chest.

Now let me be clear, my boldness wasn't always helpful, kind, or even admirable. I have been loud, brash and rude. I have been accusatory without proof, aggressive without warrant and petty without fair consideration.

Sometimes it was a front for fear, many times, it was in defiance to authority, and almost always, it was totally spontaneous, as if my Soul's Big Sister leapt up reflexively to defend me. My boldness, thankfully, has evolved over the years. It has grown out of the need to be a loud and obnoxious badass, and has matured *somewhat*, into a calm and more solid voice of confidence. (Emphasis on 'somewhat'. Progress, not perfection, is the goal.)

I have learned that tone can more powerful than volume, listening is often more useful than speaking and discernment more intelligent than wit. As I step into bigger arenas in my work, I have become very curious about my boldness and how it can be best used as a source of strength.

For a long time for me, strength meant making a witty comeback, throwing my brilliance in someone's face, being loud and making a point with the power of my voice. I thought I was demonstrating strength when I didn't shy away from cruelty, but stood strong in my rebuttal, like a lawyer in a courtroom -firm and bold, reactive and swift...like a 1-2 punch Mohammad Ali style.

I still get caught in the knee-jerk response that provokes me to speak my mind and defend my Truth. And yes, sometimes that's absolutely necessary.

What I'm learning however, through the expansion of my Soul, is that often, strength is most powerful when it rests in peace of mind.

Strength can mean refusing to play the game.

Strength is honouring the boundaries that protect my precious spirit.

Strength comes from knowing which battles are worth the bloodshed, and which will only leave me bruised and worn.

The triggers in our lives invite us into deep conversation with ourselves to explore the wounds others have bumped up

against. To ask why they still hurt. To investigate what healing is necessary. To become curious about what lessons we may have missed. This strengthens us.
Perhaps not in the eyes of the offender -no, but we can never really win matters of the soul when the result is outside of us. Strength is the deep-rooted belief that we are okay -no matter what and what my Too Bold self is learning, is that sometimes, those muscles are the ones worth flexing.

Perhaps the number one message I receive from my tribe on social media is a wish to be as bold, confident and courageous as I am. Whew. That's a helluva lot to hold, folks.

And as I sit here, typing these Big Girl words for my Big Girl book sharing my Big Girl success, I am reminded of a picture my mother took of me as a little kid, standing proudly in her high heeled shoes.

To be honest, most days, that's who I really am. A kid trying to fill a space that's too big for her.

Every time I hit 'post' on a vulnerable blog, each time I step onto a new stage to deliver a talk, every *yes* I say to an opportunity I know is well beyond my reach, I stand as the little girl in her too-big heels.

I wasn't blessed with a superior courageous gene at birth, nor do I have a secret formula for fearlessness. The truth is, *I'm scared most of the time*. Perhaps that, my friends, is the secret to my boldness.

I remember spending several days detoxing at a juicing retreat in a remote rural cottage with my best friend years ago. Beyond the extreme physical symptoms of the detox, I was riveted by an experience I had during a session with the reiki master who hosted the event.

He told me that *"I carried the sadness and longing of my maternal ancestors"* in my cells.

I collapsed into myself and cried for hours. Not from sadness, no, but from utter recognition and then from ultimate responsibility.

That experience prompted me to dig deep. Both into the history of the women who laid the genetic and energetic imprint before me, and into the core of who I was called to be. I felt obligated and privileged, to stand on the shoulders of their unrequited desires. Their bravery, their frustration, their wishes and their dreams gave me legs.

The incomparable Dr. Maya Angelou said that *"Courage is the single greatest virtue because without it, one cannot practice any other virtue."*

I don't know when my story will end, when the final curtain will close on the last performance of my life. All I know is that it's rushing by at an impossible speed. All I know is that this moment is fleeting. All I know is that, in those last breaths, I will have a moment of precious rendering when I will ask, "Have I done what I came to do? Have I lived my life to its fullest expression? Am I proud of myself and the choices I have made?"

I claim my greatest act of courage is to continue to dare to do things that fill and strengthen me, like emotional and spiritual Wheaties. My self-worth emboldens me to use my gifts and to say the unpopular thing. It builds an impenetrable shield of fortitude around my fragile ego that wants to be likeable and accepted. It double-dog-dares me every day to create the art of my soul when doubt, fear and security creep like boogeymen in the closet of my mind.

Celebrating the TOO MUCH WOMAN

I am clear that I have not been given this platform to link arms and sing you all Kum-ba-ya. I am here to use my voice to rattle the bones of comfort and complacency. To enliven hope and possibility in all who cross my path. To invite you to pause for a moment, say, *this one,* if only long enough to tap into the message alive in your cells, to hear the voices of your ancestors past and future, and to be bold enough to say yes to the call of your heart.

THE MOVEMENT

We Are Too Much Women

and we will not dim any longer

A Movement has been birthed.
Not from Ego and Glory and Facade.
But from the womb of pure connection, radiant hope and a deep reverence for the Feminine Spirit.
Gather extraordinary women, as we share our stories, our truth, our desires, laying the foundation like the path of a birth canal, for this labour of love to be born.
We are Too Much Women and we will not dim any longer.
We believe without a doubt that *every* woman is called to a particular slice of destiny that belongs to her and no one else.
We believe when a woman exquisitely honours her TOO MUCH qualities -her uniqueness -she can move mountains with her impact on the world.
We believe that the world requires her to share her gifts, in order for all of us to evolve, to heal and to co-create a new world of balance between the feminine and masculine energies.

We believe in an abundant Universe, where we celebrate and support one another, and where there is space for each of us to flourish.

Celebrating the TOO MUCH WOMAN

Gather tribe. Gather women. It's time.

At the heart of the movement and the global tour, are the Too Much Women themselves.

The following pages feature just a few of the extraordinary women I know personally, who embody the heart and ethos of the Too Much Woman philosophy. Their work, their art, their passion and their generosity of spirit has had an impact on me and many others.

I bow to each of you, my sisters. I honour the energy of you and bless the ripples you put out into the Universe. Thank you for shining so brightly, so that we may all recognize the light within ourselves.

Marlo Ellis: Too Strong

Founder and Visionary of the Uncommon Woman

www.theuncommonwoman.com

In 2011 I found myself in an abusive relationship.

It all seemed so surreal to me. It wasn't something that I had ever been exposed to, nor was it part of my blueprint. I wasn't a textbook victim of abuse. I hadn't witnessed it as a child, nor had I ever accepted it as a young woman, and certainly not as an adult. On the contrary, I came from a loving family. I had always had healthy relationships, and I was the woman who others had leaned on in times of sadness and fear. I was an expert in leading women through transformation, helping them see what wasn't working in their lives and guiding them as they implemented what would. Yet there I was in my own nightmare.

I found myself beaten and battered, not by fists but by words, unsure how to define it. He'd found a weak spot. I was coming into a new career that I loved, and this new identity was so foreign to me that his words hit me right in my vulnerability and took me out at the knees. I suddenly believed that this new person had a new perspective on the new version of me, and he saw right through me.

He found the crack in my confidence and filled it with everything he could to shatter my soul.

I was nothing without him and was lucky to have found him.

I was a disaster waiting to happen.

I was delusional if I thought I would ever get anywhere on my own.

Everything I had suspected him of was all a product of my own lies and insecurities.

I had no real expertise and was a complete fraud.

Eventually I would be found out and he would sit back and laugh.

I was just another stupid bitch who thought she had value.

And of course, because we are what we believe, it all became truth in my mind. I questioned my ability and qualifications. Every mistake I made was more proof. I questioned my expertise and played small. I spent hours trying to convince him that I was worth his time when I felt him distancing. Who was this woman? Everything that I was doing and thinking felt wrong and foreign and I hated myself for being weak, and scared. I let his dialogue become the one that played through my mind day in and day out, to the point that I could barely stand my own company.

Then I started searching for answers because I knew I was wiser than he said. I had a lifetime of evidence to prove it! Once I searched deeper, I'd found he'd had multiple affairs with both our clients and friends and suddenly all of it made sense. Separating my thoughts from what I knew to be true, I started listening. I asked questions and heard the answers.

The evidence had been there all along. He had been projecting his fears on me, and because I hadn't trusted my own voice, I fell for it.

In a moment of complete clarity and anger, I left and never looked back. It was inconvenient but it changed my life and the people I allowed into my circle.

When we don't want to see truth because of the inconvenience it may cause we choose to stay in the illusion. The moment we open to our truth, forgive our past and take responsibility for our future, our world is forever changed.

Patti M Hall: Too Intense

author. coach. ghostwriter. book architect

www.pattimhall.com

"How can I help?" the voice of the stranger on the other end of the phone asked.

Before, I would have made a sarcastic quip, desperate not to be perceived as too intense, I'd make myself cute and small, cleave to politeness and make the world-famous doctor laugh. That was my schtick, my MO. I'd been taught my place. I'd stepped back when I was told, squeezed into the supporting role of his wife, her assistant, their co-author, someone's second-in-command, and forced backstage, my entire life.

But this wasn't about me. I might have reverted to the old script if it was about me. The last vestiges of my Funny Girl veneer were gone. I'd sacrificed her in the pediatrician's office. Perhaps the part of me that would have acquiesced, afraid of being too outspoken, fearful of offending someone with my knowledge, went over the cliff's edge as I stared at a pile of my son's school pictures and wondered how the hell I'd missed the signs before.

"Tell me what you know so far," he said.

And I did.

I wedged open the crust, stepped onto the path into my son's precarious future. Just months before in Iceland, I stretched out my arms walking between the two tectonic plates, nearly able to touch the continental Before and the After, a metaphor for the irreparable cleft created by a rare disease diagnosis exploding into my son's life.

I blurted out a list of the medical facts I'd discovered in bits and pieces from doctors with specialties I would previously (and contentedly) not have known existed. I gave blood levels and tumour measurements, and when I got to the part about my son's pain, I heard my voice quake, and instead of feeling compelled to regress into apologies and disclaimers, I let him tell me that my son was lucky to have me, and that my well-informed advocacy would likely be the thing that would save his life.

I pulled on my armour, hauled my baby under my wing, and waged battle. I got a PhD in my son because there was no one who knew him as well as I did. I elbowed and crusaded my boy's way into a medical system where administrative walls were built around the most specialized physicians. I weaseled my way into referrals and used every personal connection I had to get global experts to talk to me. I beat back the judgmental and uninformed opinions: the natural supplement advocates and those hapless souls who told me about a shaman they saw on *Oprah* once who could cure anything with a rainforest bromeliad. I researched for countless hours while my boys slept, staunching the emotional wounds caused by the under-the-breath accusations of friends and extended family that I was overreacting.

Too intense for everyone else, except my sick child.

And he still shines brightly. Thank you for asking.

Katia Miller: Too Rebellious

Business and Visibility Strategist, Founder of Positive, Fabulous Women

www.katiamillar.com

Some people are born fitting in while others are meant to stand out. They are the leaders, teachers, guides and changemakers. I wish I knew that as a little girl.

I grew up as an only child, in a large, traditional, religious family. As far back as I can remember, I was different — and usually not in a good way.

School was always an interesting experience for me. While I excelled in academics and was popular amongst my peers, I always felt like an outsider. I stood out, partly because I was the only blonde girl with blue eyes in my school — but mostly because I was a rebel who resisted authority and marched to a different drumbeat.

My father worked for an airline which gave me the opportunity to travel extensively as a child and exposed me to a variety of cultures and points of view early on in life. That experience helped shape my identity and provided me with a unique perspective on the world. It was also a curse in some ways because it made it even harder for me to fit it.

At home, my mother was my harshest critic, who took it upon herself to constantly remind me of my shortcomings and challenges. There was not a day that went by where I was not compared to other "good" girls with specific areas where I needed to improve and do better.

The message I received throughout my childhood was clear. I was too much: too talkative, too rebellious, too much of a free thinker, too curious, too stubborn and simply too much to handle.

I felt like a disappointment and a failure. No matter how hard I tried, I was never good enough for the people whose approval I desperately craved.

After living in 4 countries on 3 different continents, I eventually got married and settled down in the suburbs. With a successful husband at my side, I finally felt validated and more ready than ever to fit in. I worked in the corporate world and embraced my role as a wife, and eventually a mother to my two sons.

I was living the dream. Yet I felt like a fish out of water.

It was only after the end of my marriage and the start of my entrepreneurial journey that I finally started fully accepting and embracing *all* of me. Now I know that what I perceived as flaws my entire life are actually my superpowers. My pain became my gift. My inability to fit in made me a good leader.

After a lifetime of feeling too much of one thing and not good enough of another, I was finally in a place where I was ready and willing to allow myself to just be me.

Oh, what a relief!

We are always told to live by the Golden Rule and treat others as we would like them to treat us. Now my goal is to treat myself with the same level of love and respect in which I treat others. It's not always easy. I still get tripped up every now and then and find myself judging, criticizing and beating myself for being different. Yet I continue to do the inner work and put one baby step forward to show up, connect and shine.

Tara Mullarkey: Too Needy

Embodied Coach and Business Accelerator

www.taramullarkey.com

My dad left when I was 12. At that point, as the eldest child, I had worked hard to "be the good girl" in hopes of keeping them together. I was quiet when told to be. I stuffed down my sadness and anger. I over-excelled at school.

Somehow, I thought that if I did things just right - for them - they would finally turn towards me and truly see me, and love each other. It would keep our family together.

That's quite a job for a 12-year-old.

It wasn't until a failed relationship in my mid-twenties and many more in my thirties that I started to see the patterns of co-dependency that had formed in those early years.

You see, because my parents weren't truly emotionally available for me (or each other), I learned very early to abandon my needs to please them, to be loved by them.

This is how I learned to love and be loved.

Love men who are totally unavailable and stuff down my needs to try to make them love me.

Problem is, when you stuff down your needs, they inevitably erupt from time to time.

I developed a shadow and resisted being *needy*.

I was *only* attracted to men who mirrored back that belief to me, so I often heard, "You ask for too much,"...or they left.

Then I would go in this cycle of self-doubt around my needs. And I started to hide my needs for fear I'd be rejected.

It wasn't until I began to work with mentors, coaches, and therapists, that I started to understand the reason why I wasn't attracting the kind of relationships I wanted. Men weren't showing up for me in the way I deeply desired and that sent me on a hunt to figure out why.

I began to see that I was consistently abandoning myself and my own emotional needs. I was petrified of speaking my truth, my boundaries, and my needs, for fear of being left and abandoned.

I was afraid I might be taken the wrong way or other people might get the wrong idea of me. They might think I'm a whore or a bitch. I learned they might not love me. They might abandon me. They might choose someone else to love.

I learned very cleverly how to mold myself into someone they will *hopefully* love.

The ironic thing is that it's a self-fulfilling prophecy. The more you abandon your own needs - which usually shows up as people-pleasing or being the "wallflower"- the more you will be in relationship with emotionally unavailable types.

Once you bring your "neediness" into wholeness, you no longer come across as "needy".

Being "needy" is not unhealthy. We need to heal our relationship with our needs if we desire true intimacy, connection, and self-worth - and to live a life of purpose, pleasure, and prosperity.

It is actually healthy to let the people you're in relationships with know what your needs are. This gives them a chance to meet your needs. But you must know what they are first. It all starts within….

Remember, it's never too much to ask for what you need.

Anna Tsui: Too Smart

Life and Business Coach

www.annatsui.com

Before I could talk, my mom told me I was "too smart for my own good," and she meant it. I was already reading and memorizing poetry and pointing out Chinese characters to make sentences. She was actually scared that the Chinese government would take me away into a gifted program and she would not see me again.

I had to be hidden.

When we came to the States, we lived in government housing and I went to public school. My first years here were the worst years of my life. At elementary school, my English was too remedial, and I was too slow. Some girls would wait for me in the playground and beat me up during recess because I was too foreign-looking. When I got off the school bus I had to run home to keep from being jumped. I was too easy a target.

I wish I could be hidden.

I came home with bloody noses and bruises and my mom was too scared and felt too helpless to do anything about it. My dad was too tired from working 14-hour shifts to pay much attention.

I was invisible.

I excelled at school, but I was too ashamed and scared that I would stand out and get targeted. So, I would often not study or I would act out because being too smart was not cool. At home, I stayed quiet and tried not to take up too much space. There was too much stress, too many bills, too little money and I felt responsible.

I made myself invisible.

Something snapped in me as a teenager. I dyed my hair purple and hung out with the punk rockers. All of a sudden, as if everything that I held back came bursting forth, I was too outspoken, too critical, too honest, too independent, and too unruly. I made people cry, I stole things and talked myself out of getting arrested. I told off teachers and my parents. I was getting a lot of attention from older guys. I would go out all night and skip school and get caught.

I was too visible.

In my twenties I tried too hard to please people. Everyone seemed to be on a track to success, yet I felt like I was too dumb, too ugly and too late to make something of myself. I knew I had so much to offer but I didn't know what, so I always settled for third place. I was missing something, and I tried to find it in every relationship, every job, every bit of success and every other person.

I wanted so badly for people to see me.

Now, in my thirties, I realize I don't like the feeling of settling or needing to hide who I am and what I think. All those "too much yet not enough circumstances" have created a woman that is perfectly equipped to rise to any occasion because she knows that, as long as she defines herself, the world will follow suit.

I see myself.

Rina Rovinelli: Too Controlling

Co-founder SpeakerSlam

www.speakerslam.ca

As a young girl, I watched my mother navigate her way through life, first with my abusive father, and then later, my drunken stepfather. At one point we were set to go into the city to go back-to-school shopping. We lived in a small town so those trips were always very exciting and long anticipated. My brother and I stood at the car waiting for my mother. My stepfather was drunk and belligerent. In his typical fashion, he'd decided we weren't going and had hidden the keys. My mother looked at him imploringly, her eyes silently begging him. There weren't many words exchanged and in the end we all bowed our heads and returned inside. I remember my feelings of helplessness amid the disappointment and rage. But what I remember most was her silence. My inward screams echoed through my body and yet silence surrounded me. Why didn't she stand up for herself? Why didn't she stand up for me? Why didn't she take us out of this situation?

Year after year that same song played: "this will never be me". And it wasn't. I found my voice at a very young age. I spoke up in every situation. I took the lead in every group. I controlled every relationship. I was the leader, the boss, and the controller.

Throughout my life, there have been a slew of failed relationships where the common accusation was "you're too controlling". I would shrug indifferently with zero remorse. My family would make jokes, my friends would tease me about my controlling nature and yet there wasn't much humour behind their words. For everything I gained by being controlling, there were things I was losing, but the payoff was too high to stop. One day I realized that I'd mastered controlling and that if I could shift that from controlling other people and instead focus on controlling me, my life, my situation, my circumstances, I could be super powerful. It was a skill –my super power! I just needed it to work for me instead of against me.

I've spent my life as an entrepreneur, leading my business from the helm, in full control. Whenever there are opportunities presented to me, I don't waver, I step up and take control. When I started Speaker Slam I was in the delicate position of having to balance within a partnership, but we quickly divided our roles and responsibilities so that I would have full control of my role. Because to me, control represents self-reliance, independence and the freedom to execute. We have achieved great success and we attribute that to being able to play to our strengths.

My name is Rina, and I'm too controlling. I own it proudly and it has served me well!

Eram Saeed: Too Headstrong

Founder, From Heartache to Joy Global Telesummit

www.manifestality.com, www.fromheartachetojoy.com

I only had been inside of the house for just a few minutes.

I glanced around at the bustle of activity inside the house as movers moved to and fro packing up and carrying out the items that totaled my life with my soon-to-be-ex-husband.

The divorce papers were perched on the kitchen island. All was left now was for me and my husband to sign them.

I called out to him, letting him know that I was there. I took a deep breath in, squared my shoulders, and started to head toward the kitchen, toward the waiting divorce papers, when his hand shot out of nowhere, grabbing me by the collar and before I was cognizant of what was happening, he had slammed me against a wall!

The blunt force of my body crashing against the wall knocked the wind out of me, my back instantly throbbed with pain.

Pinned up against the wall, he kept squeezing my collar until my feet were lifted a bit up off the floor. I gasped for breath, grasped futilely for my footing. And I could feel his breath, hot against my face as he screamed obscenities at me: "Who the fuck do you think you are?"

All activity halted as the movers watched us. I looked at his face. How scary it looked. This very face that I had once loved, this man who had loved me was now staring back at me with these wild eyes, eyes I couldn't even recognize. Nothing but violence and anger in them. Contorted face, unrecognizable eyes, hands at my neck, the shouting and cursing... absolute sheer terror. Terror and pain, and then horror, as I looked over to discover my three year old daughter was watching us!

My pain was nothing when I saw her. And I *knew* that something vital had been taken away from her in this moment – her sense of security, that the world is a good place, gone forever. And that thought shook me so deeply in my core that I decided to wake up!

My name is Eram Saeed, and after that assault I decided that there was no way, EVER again that would I expose either of my daughters to this type of BS. It was 2010 and this ugly scene had been the culmination to a lifetime cycle of one bully after another trying to stop me from being me. Throughout my life, I had lived out the pattern of making myself so small, small as a pin, as to not to upset others. A pattern undoubtedly imprinted during childhood, born of a culture where women are to remain quiet, obedient, unheard, unseen.

I was fed up. And MAD. And for the sake of my daughters, I had to change this story. Fast. My only safety net: Me! Seething with the rage of the mother whose children had been threatened, I set out to change the story of my life. And change it I did!

Today I am the host and founder of The Global Telesummit series called *From Heartache To Joy* which has served thousands of spiritual women across the globe for seven years. Within eighteen months of its creation, the Telesummit crossed seven figures in revenue. I teach enlightened business women how to create a life of freedom and impact. I have helped 83 graduates grow their spiritual coaching businesses, many generating six figures, starting from scratch, just as I did. Last year saw the launch of my creation, Manifestality.com, which is the world's largest database of on-demand energy healers online.

Just a short few years ago I didn't have even the slightest hope that life could be more than just hardship and crushing disappointment. Today I am living my dream life. That old game I had been playing…the one where I made myself small, pleased others, diminished this spark of Light inside me—that is inside all of us—well, it served absolutely NO ONE. I decided to be all of me, all of the time. *Am I too much?* I have been charged with being "too much" all my life. Too smart, too bold, too headstrong, too opinionated, too pretty, too outspoken. Can we be too much? As we look at the world around us today, perhaps the better questions that we should be asking ourselves are: *What more can I be? What more can I do? How can I utilize my gifts and talents to change the world more? How can I serve others more? How can I expand myself more and be of more benefit to others?*

I invite you to join me by just being YOU. Be you, all of you, all of the time. Be fully yourself, in your power, unabashedly "too much." The world needs all of you, there is no time for anything less.

Pamela Sylvan: Too Confident

MojoMaker, Mentor and Publicity Maven

www.PamelaSylvan.com

Unhappiness had burrowed deep inside me like a ground squirrel attempting to keep warm at the height of an Arctic winter. My malaise and gloom provided a fertile breeding ground for disease and illness, so it was no surprise when my health crashed.

On a particular (and last) ambulance trip to the hospital where I was now a familiar figure, I was shocked to see a barrage of attendants standing at the open ambulance doors apparently awaiting my arrival.

Unbeknownst to me at the time, I was shuttled in as a massive stroke victim. A team of doctors and nurses flew around attempting to bring down off-the-chart vascular numbers.

The world slowed down. I knew why I was here. The medical reasons were minor points, projections of the real issue. My inner world was stressed. I had brought this on by my stubborn, fear-based, unwillingness to make necessary changes in my life.

Among the hive-like activity of the hospital staff I made a promise to live. My very own intimate plea to the Almighty that if allowed to walk out, whole and healthy, I'd risk it and make the necessary changes.

A day later, along with a supreme promise to look after myself, I wheeled out of the hospital assisted by a perplexed nurse who couldn't quite understand how I managed to sidestep the inevitable. I, however, had a clue, one I would keep under wraps a bit longer.

I left, with my life intact on a clear afternoon and vowed never to mistreat it or let it go again.

Remembering the promise made that day, I set out to snatch back my life.

The first order of business: dismantle what stood in the way of my dreams, which systematically stifled my creative ambitions. My marriage had to end. I had dishonoured my still small voice years ago, and lined up alongside societal and cultural convention. Aside from a beautiful daughter, my one recurring reward for a life of quiet despair, I was climbing back from the razor's edge of death.

Yes, many would rant and rage at the life altering course I was now on, but the woman I had put aside years ago by mindlessly uttering 'I do', was clambering to reappear and reassert herself again.

It took shock trauma which came via the death of a much-loved fish named 'Blue' to catapult me across the finish line of a waning promise made only days ago. This sign from life woke me up to a dark future if I allowed fear to win.

I said my goodbyes that fateful day and headed directly into my new life.

Celebrating the TOO MUCH WOMAN

Was it easy? It was the most gut-wrenching thing I'd ever done in life, but without it, Pamela, The MojoMaker, who joyfully helps others infuse their dreams with power and clarity would not have floated into existence.

Moving across the country, alone, creating a magazine, building a PR and mentoring business, living by the ocean, writing, creating videos, hosting events, making amazing heart connections, becoming a bigger, brighter version of myself, all these were possible because I stepped down from playing life small and made the choice to stop dying and accept and live my brand of 'too muchness'.

~ excerpt from, *SNATCH Back Your Life + 39 Other Keys To Unlock Your Power and Joy*

Luckey Tyagi: Too Trusting

Writer and Speaker, Myriad Mad Musings

Founder, The Sunflower Project

https://www.instagram.com/myriadmadmusings/?hl=en

Taking a leaf out of the journal of memory land, far back from the time when I was an ebullient, outspoken, confident and bright little girl, I can recall that society-at-large snapped up and lapped up every opportunity to let me know (and not subtly) that girls and women were children of a lesser God / Goddess.

Very soon I discovered the correlation between my choosing to express my unbridled self and the raised eyebrows and open mouths of those around proclaiming me TOO MUCH.

So I began to devise hacks to not appear TOO SMART, TOO INTELLIGENT, TOO AMBITIOUS, TOO CONFIDENT, TOO INDEPENDENT, TOO LOVING, TOO GIVING, TOO EMOTIONAL, TOO STUBBORN, TOO IMAGINATIVE, TOO BOSSY, et ali.

Thus, most of my life up until my forties was spent in an invisible warzone, where my glorious, luscious, radiant, rebellious true self was constantly battling to contain itself into the pretty, pleasing box of conformity without letting any light spill out.

At one point in time, even managing to convince myself that me and my pretty box were a perfect fit, together we danced from one masquerade ball to another, the masks getting bigger to hold my smiles captive and the box getting tighter to hold my breath captive.

Until one day the box began to cut into my ribcage, going from skin deep to soul deep and I realized I was not ready to die yet. Then began the long drawn, painstaking journey of raking through the muck to release all that was not mine, to finally embrace myself, the white, the black, the grey, the blue and every other hue, except the label of being TOO TRUSTING.

Yes! I am that person who trusts people and their goodness and their integrity explicitly and implicitly.

And, yes! I'm that person who has had her heart broken into a million shards many times over and whose back is permanently scarred from being stabbed.

Yes! I was let down and cheated on in love and business and generally by people I would have gladly taken a bullet for.

So obviously, I turned bitter and was afraid of being let down again. I felt unlovable, but what really wounded deeply and made me feel small and unworthy, was the judgement from loved ones, like that I had personally failed them by allowing myself to be cheated on. Implicit accusations telling me that I was incapable of judging people, that I lacked sense and sensibility and perhaps I deserved it all for having chosen to do business with friends rather than family.

I kept wallowing in the guilt for having made the wrong choices. I began to avoid conversations about and references to these topics. Though outwardly defensive, I found it torturous to look myself in the eye. My self-esteem nose-dived completely, slowly, leading to depression, I closed myself off from people and vowed never to let anybody penetrate the fortress around my heart, I vowed to prove myself worthy of being worldly wise.

Easier said than done, for caring for people, supporting and encouraging them, lending an ear, seeing and believing in the good, connecting at a deep level are oxygen to me. I cannot live a fulfilled life without being open to people and the possibilities of connection. I had boxed myself in again and the box had begun to dig into my ribcage, until sick and tired of pretending, it dawned on me, that my worth could not be held hostage by what other people chose to do with my trust.

What had transpired were just experiences, my decisions and choices had always come from a place of love and I was only doing the best as I knew how. Whether or not other people chose to honour that love, support and trust was a reflection of them and not me.

Also, the learning that came from those experiences was a bonus, the resilience, the strength, the problem solving, the discernment, the growth all add to that halo that shimmers today as I nod my wise, worthy head.

Okay, so some friends and lovers have let me down but what about the countless friends, acquaintances and even strangers that have gone not just the extra mile, hundreds of miles, out of their way to help me and build me? Do I not owe it to them and to myself to remain, open, free of guilt and bitterness to let the magic of connection thrive.

Yes, their might be times that people will let me down again, but I am willing to take that in my stride and I remain open to endless possibilities.

Celebrating the TOO MUCH WOMAN

Finally, the last piece of the too much woman jigsaw fits and I am no longer ashamed to be too trusting.

This is a women's movement, yes.

A space for us to gather and find reprieve, to be inspired to share our gifts, to feel supported, seen and celebrated, and then ultimately, to go back out into the world and take action.

I wanted to hold a space, both literally in this book, and figuratively in the world, for the men who have shown up with sincerity, with compassion and with deep concern, to support the rise of the feminine.

There have been so many who have written to me, who have shared their own Too Much stories or the stories of their loved ones, and who have expressed a desire to do whatever they can to carry the movement forward.

Thank you. We appreciate you.

Dennis Gabrial Smith: Supporting the Rise of the Feminine

Spiritual Business Guide, Co-Founder, Oasis

https://www.oasisinnerjourneys.com

For me, as a man, this all boils down to the relationships I have in my everyday life. And in the end, the relationship I have with my Self.

I have both Feeling sensitivity, as well as Thinking sensibility, and they dance together, creating something new in this world – my Self expression.

The change is the realization that the masculine is not actually 'leading', the feminine is.

My daughter Sophia is 11 years old, soon to be 12, and I've always treated her with the understanding that she knows innately what is best for her. I don't need to program her, other than some basic life skills. As a result, she has grown up with an overpowering enthusiasm for life, whether it was digging in the dirt, running with no particular direction in mind, making up stories, or creating her own songs.

Along the way however, she met the male dominated paradigm. And it's been hard.

At first, I tried to coax her into taking private singing lessons to get ahead of the game and compete with the other parents and kids. But nope! Not for her. She slowly detached from the social systems and found herself alone on a path that she was unsure of, and it showed in her face and energy.

One day she came home and said, "Papi, sometimes I don't have anyone to play with at school. So, I sing to the trees."

Obviously, this just about broke my heart, and my first reaction was to swing this fricken' paradigm as hard as I could the other way.

Then I listened. Instead of acting on my masculine aggressive nature, I chose to believe there was a reason for this experience, for her soul. I know for myself, I went through so many challenges and so much pain, that I reached my bottom. And it was there that I found sincerity, and gave up to the higher purpose of life.

Sophia was already looking for her Destiny, and organizing opportunities around whatever she felt became her purpose. And then one day, with a smile on her face, she said, "I Found it! I'm here to sing!"

Hallelujah.

But before long, she was losing this joy, standing at attention in the choir, singing other people's songs.

"I'm quitting choir," she announced, and my heart splashed on the floor. And then, "I'm going to sing my own song at the school talent show instead."

And she did, the first act, first time, in front of 250 people on stage. She shone!

I've worked with Gina in both business and spiritual spheres before the Too Much Woman wave began and continue to do so coordinating her world events.

The message that I resonate so much with about Gina's work, is this:
Yes, there is an imbalance in our world, and right now the feminine, feeling nature is rising to bring hope and love to schools, business, health, spirituality, and the world.

But the difference is that now there is a maturity to realize these changes come from within, and they require balance. After all, the more you push a pendulum one way, the farther it will swing the other way. And instead of an age-old battle between thoughts and feelings, we can find our Cygnus, our balance, by relaxing deeper into the sincerity of our feelings, and use the power of our minds to create more opportunity and change.

And to quote my daughter Sophia, "Sometimes the Jaguar sings, and the Birds roar, it's still not a mixed-up world."

I look forward to the deep Spiritual work coming, as we Balance this world, from Within.

Sips

Beautiful Souls,

I want to tell you a brief story about a girl.

She was a volcano.

Irrepressible passion, bold defiance, fierce love, immeasurable curiosity, boundless hope.

All of it bubbling, waves upon waves of it, erupting from within and wanting *out*.

So one day, she started a tiny blog on a page, and she wrote.

She wrote to acknowledge and release the creative spirit that longed to commune with the sun and the stars, and to satiate those who were hungry for her bread, aching for her medicine.

It was an audacious move. Reckless and bold and presumptuous.

All art is.

To begin the slow and vulnerable strip tease performance where masks, lies and perfection lay in a heap discarded, and where her thick, thunderous thighs were displayed as truths exposed for all to see.

Celebrating the TOO MUCH WOMAN

And she wrote.

And her tribe gathered slowly and steadily.

And their presence inspired her, healed her, stretched her, affirmed her.

And, heart bursting, she wrote.

For the past few years, I have shared slices of myself on my Facebook page.

Cautiously at first, and then with your encouragement and a splash of daring, with more honesty and abandon.

It is somewhere in these musings, that I found my Too Much voice.

I am so grateful for the opportunity to express, curate and refine my creativity in such a loving and supportive space.

Thank you to each of you for your likes, heartfelt comments and constant sharing of my work.

And thank you for asking me to assemble a collection of my writing for you to have and hold, to ponder and play with, to revisit and reflect upon. I am finally ready.

Your Ask is the most loving gift you have given me.

My hope is that these words expand your heart, inspire your imagination and give legs to your courage.

May your cup be full my loves. Know I am with you every sip of the way!

Gina

Because Your Life Is For You

I don't know why I did it.
I just know that I couldn't NOT do it.

I spontaneously entered a speaking contest and then, told the truth.

For the record, I haven't been in a speaking contest since the 8th grade.

For the record, I haven't told this truth in all my life.

For the record, I didn't ask for any of this.

They say when the student is ready, the teacher appears.

Seems my teacher was an opportunity.

I've worked as a speaker since I left my job as a journalist 23 years ago (don't hurt yourself on the math…just trust me).

But *this* time, *this* speech, *this* stage was different.

It wasn't a talk for a corporate client, or one written to empower participants at a workshop, or a talk for a gym full of high school kids or even a talk prepared for a riveting keynote.

This talk was for Me.

It wrote itself just a few days before the competition. And the words were committed to memory in a few hours.

That's how Truth flows.

Now the Truth can be very convincing...and so can I.

But truly, I don't see that as my role.

Not at all.

The energy of my Soul does not want to corner yours in a dark alley and force you to believe.

My Spirit is here to soar high in the clouds.

To be a model of the heights of possibility within you and the power of resilience when the wind currents beat you down.

My Spirit wants to 'remind' you, (literally inviting you BACK to your mind), that you are seeded in Divinity.

That you are not lacking or broken.

That our life experience is not random or whimsical.

That Life is Responding to You.

That Life is Unfolding According to You.

That Life is FOR You.

Because when you really, truly understood that, it will make me irrelevant.

And the best teachers get out of the way.

So tell me...

How would you show up in your life – TODAY – if you believed, if you remembered, that Life is For You?

That you are infinitely supported, guided and loved, even when the evidence appears to the contrary.

What would be different about your energy, your thoughts, your words, your actions if you knew this to be true?

Because, Darling, it is.

My Life Is My Art

I don't paint or draw or make music.

I don't craft or stitch or knit.

You won't see my work displayed proudly on any wall for the world to ogle and gawk at, no.

My Life is my Art.

A splash of Intention, a dab of Discomfort, a dramatic sweep of Resilience and Deep Faith.

The colours are too bold, uncomfortably dramatic and to the untrained eye, seem random and childish.

But the Red is my Love. Deep and intense.

The Orange is my Purpose. Incessant and focused. A sunrise emerging on the horizon.

The Blue is my Depth. Spiritually inclined, ever searching, mysterious.

The Yellow is my Faith. Sometimes pale, other times bright, often blinding.

The Green is my Connection to Mother Earth. A groundedness in who I am and all that I am as part of the Whole.

The Purple is my Ancestors. A lineage of strength, resilience. A wound intent on healing.

Every day I awaken to a blank canvas.

What shall I create today?

What experience will come to life when I mix the Blue and Orange? The Red and Yellow?

What masterpiece will emerge through my Creativity and Inspiration?

What great work of art will I leave as my legacy?

My life is my art.

And so is yours.

Never Tell a Too Much Woman to…

Never tell a Too Much Woman to simmer down, take it easy or "Relax, Little Lady."

Never tell a Too Much Woman to behave, "know your place" or bite her tongue unless she has proof.

Save your breath.

There's no point in wanting her to dim it, play nice or tuck herself in neatly, like the fitted sheets you lay her down on to have your way with her.

Don't shush her, or try to shame her, or even imagine for a second that there is a box big enough to hold all that she is.

She won't be silenced, despite all the tape you slap on her too much mouth, or the gag you place on her too much words.

Her Truth screams from her cells, and ricochets off of every glass ceiling and off the walls of lies you have built to keep her out of the game of life.

In the riveting words of Marianne Williamson, "Womanhood is being recast, and we're pregnant, en masse, giving birth to our own redemption."

So, "Shhhh. Bite your tongue."

Sit back in your chair. Put your seat belt on. Prepare for the ride of your life.

There is no taming the Lioness.

She has awoken.
And bedtime ain't coming any time soon.

Fear is the Best Storyteller

Up until a year ago, I resisted posting a selfie on my business page.

I thought it was shameless and I wanted my work to be about my writing.

I thought I'd be judged. Not taken seriously. Or worse–liked for superficial reasons.

For years as a speaker, particularly with men in my corporate audiences, I dressed the part.

Masculine business suits, no skin exposed, modest hair in a bun. I even bought prescription-free glasses, to "look smart." Ha.

In so many areas of my life, Fear took me out of myself and had me masquerading as someone else.

Fear told me being me was dangerous, risky, unpopular and would turn people off.

Fear told me the showing up as Gina would be a threat to my reputation and success.

Fear told me smart girls couldn't be attractive.
Respectable girls aren't sexy.
And good girls are not allowed to have too much fun.

Fear's a bitch and a fabulous storyteller.

I declare my love for Fear and all the ways it has shown up to scare the crap out of me.

Thank you fear for showing up as Failure so I could see how resilient I am.

Thank you fear for showing up as Loneliness so I could learn how much I enjoy my own company.

Thank you fear for showing up as Betrayal, so I could more fully trust myself.

Thank you fear for showing up as Rejection so I could feel full acceptance from myself.

Thank you fear for showing up as Perfection so I could know that I am enough as I am.

Thank you fear for showing up as Vulnerability so that despite being weak at the knees, I can still choose to run down the Boogeyman, grab the damn pen and write my own story.

Spiritual Growth Comes on The Wind

Contrary to popular belief, Spiritual growth doesn't come with a menu and table service.

God isn't the waiter and S/He doesn't take special dietary requests from the kitchen.

The Soup of the Day is gonna be different for everyone and not necessarily what you thought you ordered.

Basically, if you're hungry enough, you don't ask questions. You just open your mouth and eat.

I remember this time last year, I asked for Direction and Clarity and Confidence.

I felt like a raft rushing down a wild river.
I couldn't steer or even see clearly where I needed to go and I was white-knuckling the whole ride.

I THOUGHT what I was asking for was a GPS and someone with an annoying voice who would navigate the play-by-play for me.

I THOUGHT what I'd get would be akin to the Lion's Badge of Courage in the Wizard of Oz. Something I could pin on my chest that would endow me with instantaneous Bravery and Zeal.

What I got was a hurricane, tornado and tsunami.

I got twists and turns, bumps and bruises, and a ton of heart-in-my-throat moments where I desperately cried "Mercy!" to the Universe.

I resented my ask.
I questioned Her/His mercy.
I felt like my whole intention got Lost in Translation.

"Hey! You no speaka de English?!"

Now I lay bedraggled, bloody and naked upon the shore, I don't know whether to laugh with relief, or cry in frustration.

So, I do both. The laugh-cry.

I see that I could not have found this place where I have arrived by walking lightly on a paved path or even gliding on a sailboat. Or by jet, parachute or dirt bike.

The only method of transportation was to be carried on the wind.
In surrender and faith.

And I can see more clearly now, the rain is gone.

I Detest Being Controlled

There is an innate, wild rebellion that stirs within me when I feel the slightest tug on my tethered spirit.

Like a harness, I feel a constriction on my sense of freedom and individuality, and the unbroken stallion in me instinctively pulls away.

And yet, and yet...

As I grow in my awareness, I realize daily, hmmm, almost hourly, how tied I am to my story.

Like a broken record, I repeat unconscious stories about Life Being Hard, Good Girls Always Putting Themselves Last and Money is Evil and Fleeting.

These beliefs skip over and over and threaten to jeopardize my momentum and peace of mind.

And I'm so over that.

Rolling my eyes like a rebellious teen, I am sick of hearing No Pain No Gain and Money Doesn't Grow On Trees...

I have evidence to the contrary and I am dedicating my energy to releasing all the stories of fear and lack and limitation that keep me on a leash to my past.

It doesn't have to be painful or difficult (that's a story too), it's simply a moment to moment choice to affirm a new belief that:

Life is always working in my favour

and everything in this moment is freaking Perfect.

Now, that record can skip all it wants.

What story do you choose to release?

People and Their Dreams Are My Weakness

I met Anthony and Hani in Krakow when they served me the world's best falafel wrap in the old Jewish Quarter last summer.

They are two cousins from Lebanon who left their families to come to Poland for a better life.

I was exhausted and starved after a 3 day speaking event, but I was determined to see the city.

Their smiles and evident joy melted my heart.

You see, I have a weakness.

Aside from a knock-your-socks-off kiss, a hot cuppa coffee and an endless stretch of sandy beach, I have a weakness for people and their dreams.

My heart melts at the dawn of Hope in your eyes.

I want you to make it.
I REALLY want you to make it.

The pilot light within you, no matter how dim, looks at me with pleading eyes when you speak.

"Please, pay attention to me.
See me.
Ignore the words I foolishly mutter.
Look beyond the mask I wear.
Don't forsake me.
Don't abandon me.
I'm in here.
I haven't given up...not completely. "

And so I say to you...
I see you, friend.

In your darkness.
In your frustration and confusion.
In your puddle of limitation and self-doubt.

I see you.
I see your dream and your possibility.

You are astonishing. Yes, you.

And I will hold space for you as you muddle through your questions and fury and forgetfulness.
These are all necessary.

I will hold space for you until you remember yourself.
Until you come back to your light.

I will wait here.
With patience and with love.
I see you.

Do Right By Yourself

> "You will find you don't need to trust others
>
> as much as you need to trust yourself to make the right choices."
>
> —Don Miguel Ruiz

Do you trust YOU?

I've decided that Peace of Mind trumps all other desires on my list...yup–ALL Desires.

I want to feel un-knotted.

My thoughts smooth like butter...
My shoulders relaxed and soft...
My breath effortless and rhythmic like a love song...

I've explored many paths to the Land of Peace of Mind.

Ceaseless Planning.
Hard Work.
Speaking my Opinions Loudly.
Avoiding Pain.

All dead ends. Leading nowhere purposeful or reliable.

Leading to more endless, winding paths that have me dazed and confused as I circle back to the same old lessons and frustrations.

Tightening the grip on my life squeezes out all the juicy bits. Leaving me with only the pulp.

While it is good to clean out the crap in your system, it doesn't create radiance or bliss.

Like Dorothy searching for Oz, I've had to stop seeking and stand still enough to wriggle my toes in those ruby slippers and Trust in the Power they wield.

I can't trust anything outside of me.
Everything and everyone is as free as the wind to blow this way or that.

The only true power I yield is standing in a space of Trust for Myself.

(read that over to yourself 508 times)

In any given moment I will Do Right by Gina.

In any situation I will make the choice that is born from my Higher Self.

No matter how the winds of change blow, I will steady myself, plant those thighs firmly and stand in Mountain Pose for myself and my Truth.

This is where my focus lies. In cultivating Trust in Me.

Knowing that I've got my own back and Peace of Mind is just 3 clicks of my heels away.

You'll Never Get Full On Crumbs

We all show up to the Buffet of Desire in our own way.

Some of us by habit.
Looking at the clock of our lives and deciding, "Now, It's Time For Me."

Some of us wake up ravenous, insatiable; craving what we've missed and stuffing ourselves, as our taste buds burst with all that resembles Love, Joy, Peace, Connection.

Filling plates of it to ensure we get our money's worth before the bill comes.
Jamming in mouthful after mouthful without breath, lest we waste any more precious time.

Some of us come to the buffet H*angry*.

Growling with hunger, miserable and resentful.

Waiting patiently for our meal that took forever to come, and when it does, realizing it's not at all what we craved in the first place.

Enviously eyeballing everyone else's plates and fuming that we weren't all offered the same menu items or daily specials.

Feeling slighted, cheated and silently praying that dessert will make everything okay.

Most of us were told to tame our Hunger. To stuff our Desires.

We were told our cravings were wrong and shameful.

We evolved into anorexic existences, starving the cravings of our Souls.

Swallowing the crumbs of life.

The good paying job.
The nice guy.
The knee length skirt.
The economical car.
The quiet life.
The kind words.

Silently drooling over the pastries in the window and hiding The Deep, Thunderous Growl in our stomachs, crying for MORE.

My mission is simple.
No one goes hungry on my watch.

I want you full.
I want you to burp.
I want you to devour to your heart's content. Minus the shame and guilt.

Nothing is healed or loved properly by a woman who is ravenous.

May we all rise from the table full, brimming with nourishment and joy.

That's my mission.
I want you to eat.

This is a Fundamental Truth: Nobody else can make you happy.

If you are knee-deep in self-loathing, if you are stuck in a rage of unforgiveness, if there is a part of you that can't get beyond the hurt or sadness...

No one else can fix you.

They can provide comfort, support and love, but the work and the healing needs to come from a place inside.

Even if Prince Charming rode up on his horse (in a way that wasn't creepy), his love could never fill the hole in your heart that needs attention.

Only you can do that.

The good news is that the same is true for everyone else too.

You are not responsible for their happiness. (yay!)

You are also "off the hook."

Yes, you can provide comfort, support and love, but their happiness depends on them.

(All the martyrs out there, read that sentence again.)

So if we're all off the hook (woohoo!) and everyone just took that energy of responsibility and turned it inward,

What would happen?

Hmmmm...
Sweet relief. Sweet magic.

We would all meet one another without pressure or resentment or desperation.

We would stand Mountain to Mountain in our own power.

We would unite our forces for the greater good.

So go "unhook" someone who's wasting precious energy trying to "fix it" for you.

And then,
And then...Darling,
Go unhook Yourself.

Do You Crave a Long life?

One of the first questions that is asked when someone passes is, "How old was she?"

And if the age is relatively young, we respond with a solemn head shake and breathless "Gone too soon." And if the person had lived to a ripe old age, we take some comfort in the fact that they enjoyed a long life.

Longevity is important to our human tribe.

We feel triumphant when we beat the statistical odds for average life span and can enjoy our retirement years.

Many people take medication or adjust their diet and lifestyle to extend their stay on this earthly plane...hoping for more time.

Reflecting on those in my life who have passed, both quite young and quite old, I see the importance of shifting my focus.

Being transfixed on the length of your life can be so limiting.

70 years, 85, 102...please, oh please!

We have so little control in this space, so, why waste energy here?

Gina Hatzis

What if we focused on living the WIDTH of our lives instead of the length?

Taking big chances, speaking our Truth, laughing out loud, dancing wildly, taking bold action, kissing like we mean it, baring our souls, traveling abroad, seeking deep connection, risking naked vulnerability.

I want a Wide life.

A life that covers a range of feelings and experiences and people.

A life that is unapologetic in the moments before death.

A life that makes me breathless and keeps my goose bumps on high alert.

A life that inspires others to examine and challenge the breadth of their own lives and stirs their imagination.

I want a wide life.

I choose that.

Swimming across the surface of an expansive body of water without ever diving deep to examine the treasures that long to be unearthed and celebrated, sounds dreadfully mundane.

Dive in, Darling.
Go deep.
Forget the destination marker.

Trail off the path and live wide.
Go wide.
Then wider.

Life Lessons Summed Up

I can sum up my life lessons: The Good, The Bad and The Ugly into one 5-letter word: Trust.

Trust that the Good is enough as is.
That there is nothing else you need.
That you miss out on the juiciness of life when you aren't in appreciation of what IS right now.

Trust that the Bad isn't bad.
Say what?
The Bad is contrast. It is there to illuminate the good that you have become accustomed to. It is a gift from the Universe for you to open and explore and appreciate.

Trust that even the Ugly is beautiful.
Ahhh, this one needs to be taken in small bites.

The Ugly is your Goliath.
The big kahuna.
The lesson that double-dog-dares your David to show up and hold sacred ground over your Soul.

Trust that the Universe's timing is perfect.
It knows when you are ready for your Goliath to show up.
It knows that you have all the tools, experience and courage you need to handle yourself.

Gina Hatzis

The Universe has complete faith in you to persevere.

It wants you to prevail.
It knows you can win.
It would not set you up for failure.

Trust that when you stand before your Goliath, your time is now.

You have been called.
You are ready.

Be grateful that the Universe has such faith in you.
Gain strength from that knowledge.

And then breathe deep and let your David do what needs to be done.

The Final Question Answered

"Do not go gentle into that good night,
Old age should burn and rave at close of day;
Rage, rage against the dying of the light."
–Dylan Thomas

Had a close call on the road yesterday...and it got me thinking.

I don't know when my story will end, when the final curtain will close on the last performance of my life.

All I know, is that it's all rushing by at an impossible speed.

All I know is that, this moment is utterly precious.

All I know is that, in those last breaths, I will have a moment of precious rendering.

I will ask, have I done what I came to do?

Have I lived my life to its fullest expression?

Did I leave it all on the dance floor?

Did truth spill from my lips?

And I am deciding, in this sweet moment, that my answer will be, it MUST be,

A resounding Yes!

Put Your Blinders On, Babe

Our family was taking a mini vacation in Montreal, Canada.

We donned our tourist attire and fuelled ourselves on poutine.

As we walked down a beautiful cobblestone street, we were passed by a horse and buggy.

The horse was draped in a garland of flowers and pulled young lovers along like a scene out of a movie.

My daughter pointed out that the horse had weird sunglasses on and asked me to explain.

"Oh, those are blinders. They keep the horse focused ahead instead of being distracted by what's around him." I told her.

My daughter, like all kids, made a brilliant, obvious point.

"Oh cool, they should make those for people."

Huh.

I confess, I could definitely use a pair at times.

I often get distracted, pulled out of focus and side-lined by what's going on around me- especially when it has to do with other people and my opinion of them.

When that happens, not only do I waste precious energy on things I cannot control, but it excuses me from owning my own shit.

Imagine for a moment, we all just focused on our own pile of dung.

Imagine each one of us putting our blinders on simultaneously and dealing with the stank we have created instead of wasting time complaining about the stench of being downwind from others'.

It's hard work owning your stuff.
Not excusing.
Explaining.
Ignoring.
Deflecting.

What if each of us just stuck a monogrammed flag right on top of our pile, declaring "mine"?

Now, don't be tempted to compare your pile with the next person's or play the victim for how you got stuck with yours.

Don't complain about the economy or blame your genes or focus on what he said and what she didn't do.

None of that will change a thing.

Take responsibility.
Own it... all of it.

And if it helps,
Put your blinders on, babe.

Putting Yourself Out There Can Feel Really Shitty

I've been slammed, blocked, and shamed for exposing the truth of me....

Called crass, crude, a whale, oh! and "Satan's Little Helper." What a ride, y'all!

In all fairness, 98% is all love and affirmation! Thank you!

And...

I'm still learning.

I'm still learning that when I create, it has to be For me and From me.

Born from the most authentic part of me that wants to speak my truth, explore my curiosity and spark a meaningful conversation.

I'm still learning that what others think of me is none of my business- even when it feels personal and even when it stings.

I'm still learning that Being of Service doesn't mean giving people what you think they need, but sharing what I need or have needed and then allowing people to step up and reach out if it speaks to their soul.

I'm still learning that my worth isn't tied to anyone's acceptance of me.

My worth is inherent.
It's my birthright.

And it exists independent of what anyone else says.

It is even independent of what I do, how much I accomplish and if I impact the world at all.

I'm still learning to be okay with imperfection and vulnerability and visibility.

And as long as I'm still learning all of these exquisite (albeit uncomfortable) lessons, I know I am growing. And it is worth it.

Because at the end of the day, a peach can only ripen to its fullest, juiciest potential when it's out on the limb.

And that's where I choose to hang.

Anyone dare to hang with me?

Choose To Live Impossibly

When you make a decision to colour outside the lines of convention and do things they say cannot be done.

When you become what you are told you cannot be.

When you live in a way that rejects the rules they have imprisoned you with.

Something changes in you when you turn off the radio of voices around you and tune into the music of your soul and the rhythm of your heart.

When your animal spirit howls your truth and growls away your fears.

When you climb out on the cliff of your awareness and marvel at the infinite possibilities for your life and intentionally choose magic and joy as your constant companions.

Suddenly you are in control.

You are grounded by roots that reach the centre of the Earth and a spirit that spans the Universe, and all the world conspires to support you.

It is a beautiful thing.
It is magic.
It is possible.
And it is only a choice away.

I Believe In Magic

As a former magician, I know every trick in the book.

There is no slight-of-hand more impressive than an authentic connection between Souls...

No optical illusion more powerful than witnessing someone blossom from your love...

Nothing more awe inspiring than stepping into the river of synchronicity where the Universe lines up the people, opportunities and insights in perfect time for your dream to unfold ...

No trick is more captivating than connecting to the power and inspiration that swells from the Spirit within and moves a soul to create something that never existed before.

The only magic words you need to utter are,

"Thank you, thank you, thank you!"

Then hold on to your seats and prepare to be dazzled.

Loving With All My Heart

I woke up to a flood of love.

I woke up with bifocals attached to my face.

Things just got really clear and my focus is razor sharp.

I Feel the energy of love surrounding me and don't need one more iota of proof that Love is the greatest force in the Universe!

I See beauty and hope and possibility magnified in all things …like the scene in The Wizard of Oz when it goes from black and white to technicolour.

I Know in the most desolate and skeptical crevices of my Ego that I am connected to an all-powerful force that loves me and wants only the best for me, no matter how imperfect things may seem.

I Believe in love and humanity…deeply.

And in the innate goodness of people, despite whatever the fuck the news reports.

I forgive everyone everything and wipe the slate clean…even those that have hurt me and even myself.

I trust new beginnings.
I trust life.
I trust love.
I trust Myself.

I trust the confusion and the pain and how wrong things may seem on the surface, with a steady faith that this is the Path.

This IS the path of Revolution.

I Love with all my heart.
I choose love in every form.
Not just when it feels good and it is reciprocated and I want to.

But love when it hurts, love when I'm angry, love when I'm tired and love when I don't even believe in it.

As I swim in this glorious river of rainbows and fly in these clouds with farting Unicorns, I can laugh knowing that the world is exactly what I say it is.

And today, it's freaking beautiful

I am in love with all of you.
Thank you. Thank you. Thank you.

Things Do Go Wrong

Thing go wrong. Horribly wrong.

Mistakes happen.

You get sick, someone else gets sick.
Relationships end. People die. Money is lost.

There's a flawed assumption that when things 'go wrong', that we are somehow off our path or out of alignment.

This self-flagellating belief misses the mark on a Universal Truth that you are never in fact, Off Your Path.

To ignore your very human experience of pain, loss, sadness or rejection is to dismiss the value of contrast.

Yes, wouldn't it be nice to be in a constant state of joy, awareness, gratitude and love?

Wouldn't it be just fabulous to experience no negative emotion whatsoever?

And yet, to dismiss the human experience that shapes our values, gives form and clarity to our needs and provides momentum for our actions is to miss the whole point.

Trust life.

Celebrating the TOO MUCH WOMAN

Every warm sunbeam, every cloudy shadow, every threatening bolt of lightning, every hopeful rainbow, every grumbling warning of thunder.

When you come upon your season of Knowing and you have arrived on the other side, you will understand the value of every pain, every agonized cry, every moment of unspeakable confusion you have had along the way.

You will stand triumphant in a field of faith, where each and every experience has brought you to that moment, and you will see there could have been no other way.

You will fall on your knees in gratitude for Everything.

Everything.

And looking back, you'll see how perfect the path was.

Life Is What I Say It Is

I don't need to chase life or abundance or success or love or acceptance.

I am worthy of joy and ecstasy, rest and day dreaming, long bubble baths, longer kisses, dance breaks and ice cream cones, a date with nature, with a book, with my breath.

I am the master of Time, not its slave.

I am the creator, the author and the sculptor of my life.

Joy is my mistress, my muse, my twin flame.

Because I say so, and I am the Queen of my life Kingdom.

Because I am drunk on the liquor of self governance.

Because I have earned my serenity.

Because a woman in love with her soul rules from a glorious place of compassion and kindness, patience and authentic power.

Because this is how we heal the world, through healing ourselves first.

So hold my calls, my cares, my clothes.

I'm busy.

Questioning the Life School Curriculum

At this stage in my life, the Life School curriculum has me questioning Everything.

Everything.

What I have learned about happiness, success, connection, love and purpose is being challenged, ripped apart and reconfigured like a bad nose job.

It has me looking in the mirror and not quite recognizing the Before Me and who I thought I was in that old world.

It has me stripping down to my skivvies and reassessing the woman I want to be and what clothes match who I Really Am as opposed to what the style du jour dictates.

There is much to unlearn. What exciting times!

To not only be open to new ways of being and living, but to author the story that is the Book of My Truth.

I see a new beginning coming to me...and I'm running toward it with open arms ⌧

Ya coming?

Love Is About Release

You know the saying, "you can lead a horse to water, but you can't make it drink?"

I hate the saying. Because it's so damn true.

One of the hardest things about pursuing the Journey of the Soul is not being able to take someone with you.

No matter the strength of your love or power of your intention, you just can't want something for someone more than they want it for themselves.

And
That
Sucks.

When love and loyalty keep you tethered to a soul who's unwilling to move, the weight of their anchor can drown you too.

And there's no heroism in that.

But we continue to hold on to a responsibility that isn't ours. A choice that's not in our power to make.

We must be willing to release the shackles of want for someone else and recognize that it's only by Saving Ourselves that we can offer any hope at all.

So when you feel the tug, the ache, the longing that pulls you into that space, take that loving intention, ball it up and place it in your heart.

Allow it to seed, take root and grow within you.

See it strengthening your focus and deepening your resolve.

This is the Best way, the *only* way sometimes, to inspire change in someone you love.

Be the example. Set them free. Love them anyway.

Love is not about saving a soul.
Love is embodied in the joy of witnessing a soul save themself.

Today's focus is sweet, guilt free release.

Change the World by Changing You

Nobody wants to hear this.
Not even me.

And yet, as we swim in a sea of expert opinions, finger pointing and mass frustration, I'm 'bout to stir the pot.

Everything we experience is a reflection of what we believe about ourselves.

Everything.

We simply can't outperform our level of self-confidence.

We can't call into our lives more than we think we deserve.

We can't expect a blessing and marinate in unworthiness.

The work begins within.

Stand guard at the doorway of your mind and only invite inside the guests whose company you truly desire in your life.

There is no sense going out and trying to "change the world", the system or the guy.

Everyone wants to "change the world", yet who's willing to change themself?

Celebrating the TOO MUCH WOMAN

The old paradigm of Newtonian science is dead.

There is nothing Out There to change, my friend.

The world is a reflection of Who We Are.
It's a projection of our Innermost State.

We change the world by Changing Ourselves.
Individually and then, collectively.

As we change, the world changes.

Wanna Make a Difference?
Heal thyself.

You Are Not Alone

As I write this, I am fully aware that most people won't get it.

That's okay with me.

I write this not for the sheep, the asleep or the fear mongers.

I write this for me and for You. The You's out there who are stepping up in a big way.

I write this for the souls that, whether by choice or by force, are being Uprooted.

I write this for those of us that once believed life was supposed to be neat and tidy, delivered in a box with bow.

But we know better now.

We understand that transformation is messy and uncomfortable and requires us to get Naked.

It means people will look and stare and shake their heads in disapproval.

It exposes a 360 degree view of all of our parts so that the Light can touch and Heal all of it.

Celebrating the TOO MUCH WOMAN

It requires us not to shy away from the demons but to look them boldly in the eyes and open our arms to them.

And to survive this wondrous journey, it begs us to be present enough to receive the gifts of our truth.

We are built from self respect, grace and soul, and we will not be broken.

Whatever you are facing...the You's who are reading this...

Whatever feels insurmountable and overwhelming...

May you feel the warmth of our presence.
All of us travelling this same path.

And know you are being held. And know you are not alone.

And know it is worth it.
It is so freaking worth it.

Show Up Just As You Are

Just. show. up. As you are.

I don't need you happy or pretty or part of the Polly-Anna Positive Club.

You don't need to have hit any milestone on your spiritual journey or even be on a journey at all.

Just. Show. Up.

I wanna see YOU.

Messy, windblown, confused, imperfect, snotty.

I wanna know you as you are.

Real to the core.

Wherever and however you are, is enough for me.

If I come to love your soul as it masquerades in fancy beads and tantalizing masks, I am not loving you at all.

Just show up.
Show the fuck up.

The real you.

Test me. I can withstand anything, everything you have hidden.

I won't break your gaze. I won't turn away. I won't flinch. I won't run.

I will allow my heart, my arms, my eyes to remain open so you feel unconditional love.

Unbounded acceptance.

Unfounded affirmation.

Let's hold sacred space for what is Real in this imaginary world of fakery and allow one another the golden opportunity to be Seen as we are.

Just show up for me.

I'll hold the door open for you and let you inside this cocoon of nakedness where you and I can just relax and Be.

Where your Exhale can be longer than the Inhale and you can rest. Finally. In Yourself.

Sweet Soul, all I ask, is that You Show Up.

Mid-life Crisis or Mid-life Crossroads?

Bitterness.

Usually when a women approaches a milestone birthday, say 30, 40, 50, she is confronted with 2 choices:

enthusiastically embrace the next chapter of her story, OR get muddled in the bitterness of 'should haves', could haves' and 'what-the-f-was-I-thinkings'.

This choice, whether conscious or subconscious, accepted or denied, is pivotal in setting her course emotionally.

It's the difference between a Crisis and a Crossroads at middle-age.

By this point in your life you have probably been shit-on, dumped, betrayed, abused, and disappointed. You've been laid off, passed over for the job or promotion, underappreciated, ignored, left behind by people who have died, been stuck with the wrong people who have lived. You have witnessed more sadness, unfairness and politics and drama than you can bear...

And yet, and yet, at mid-life, you realize an amazing thing.

You. Have. A. Choice.

Celebrating the TOO MUCH WOMAN

You come to see how easy it would be succumb to bitterness. No one would blame you for it.

(The world sucks, right?)
Look no further than the news, our food, the environment, the education system, the cray-cray comments on Facebook.

Or…you can choose another way. You can slow way the hell down.

You can focus on the juicy goodness of the first crisp apple of the season, the way the spring promises new life and delivers–every time, the hug of a friend who knows your ugly side and stays, the laughter of an inside joke, the smell of the body that chose you to share the bed with, the breath that continues to come up whether you are laughing, crying, screaming or snoring.

You can choose. Oh how you can choose!

Yes. You can choose.

Crisis or Crossroads. Dare to decide.

Where Are You Ecstasy?

Ecstasy. You are mine. I own you. This moment is ours.

Bliss. Elation. Euphoria. Rapture.

I have flirted with your posse.
Toyed with your lesser-than brethren.
Danced around the perimeter of your likeness.

And none was enough. I want you.

Ecstasy.

My birthright. Home to my Soul. Joy of all joys.

I have run myself ragged trying to find you. To locate you on the map of my life.
Searching with a flashlight to find you in my trepid unworthiness.

After all, They Said you were Out There.

Amidst security and piles of money
Glowing in my Twin Flame's undying love
Or beneath a pile of degrees, achievements and other worldly successes

But Ecstasy…I looked in all those places and you were not there.

All I found were breadcrumbs of Not-Enough-ness and Conditional Love, and a stale crust of Co-Dependence.

Not enough sustenance to quell the hunger of my Soul.

Ecstasy. Where could you be? And why would God hide you in the most unfathomable place?

Why the never-ending, un-figure-out-able mystery, the Hide-and-Seek game that never, ever ends.

What fun is there in that?

So I call off the search and just Be. JUST BE. And announce that I'm through chasing you.

I surrender. I will be okay with okay. It will suffice.

And I breathe into that space. I give it all up.

And then I look up. And wouldn't ya know it.

There You Are.

Today Can Be Your Day

I've got about 49 open tabs in my brain and a Future demanding me to resolve them.

A tsunami often hits without much warning and doesn't ask for permission.

It laughs at days on a calendar, deadlines and my body's desperate plea for rest.

But it also doesn't know me.

And the power of my boundary.
The fortress I am learning to build around my needs.
The guard dog at the door to my inner peace.

It doesn't know about my ally, Sunday.

Sunday who doesn't ask.

Sunday who lets me Be.

On Sundays I stop moving and plant my feet Here.

I allow all the spaces within me – depleted from a week of output – to slowly fill back in.

On Sunday I go slow.

Celebrating the TOO MUCH WOMAN

I breathe with intention.

Allow the coffee to swirl on my tongue a second longer.

Hold my smile until it reaches my eyes.

Let my exhale extend beyond my inhale.

Today I don't need answers and I won't ask questions.

Today it will be enough to Be.

To observe without judgment.
To see without attaching.
To love without condition.
To sit without guilt.
To sigh without reason.
To laugh without a joke.
To feel peace without resolution.
To trust without proof.

This will be my day.

Clarity Does Come

Sipping from my Cup 'o Clarity this morning

Yesterday was a game-changer for me.

Ever have one of those days?

When the lessons are mammoth, obvious and relentless?

When there is no sheepish hiding behind the "Well, maybe..." messages from the Universe.

When Spirit looks you square in the eye, grabs you by the shoulders and says Listen!

When things come clearly into focus like wipers clearing the windshield from the rain of confusion.

Or when you were a kid connecting the seemingly random dots on the page and suddenly the picture appears before your eyes...Voila!

Ahh yes, one of those days.

When all I can do is sit with my mouth open and wonder at how everything fits.

How even the unfinished picture and unanswered questions make sense.

And how I still don't know what I'll do tomorrow but that's okay. It's all okay. It's gonna be okay.

It's one of those days.

And I hardly want to close my eyes and risk the clarity fading by dawn.

But knowing that closing my fist too tightly will squeeze the life out of this energy.

I know I need to release and trust.

I guess that's why I document it.

Proof that, if only for a brief moment in time,

everything is truly perfect

I don't have to like it, or be a victim to it or resist it.

I can just take small sips from my cup and make peace with it.

And in that space, trust I'll know the Next Best Thing to do.

Honour That Younger You

There She is.

Yesterday, I was adding my daughter's grade 7 school picture to her album...and found myself flitting through photos for quite some time.

She's been at it.
Hustling at school: the Track team, Glee club, challenging academic program, and the 5 hours of dance per day.

I was so full of love for the way she's "All In" in life, at the beauty of her Becoming and her unbelievable journey so far.

I was marinating in complete adoration of her and all the dreams I have for Her – until I came across a picture of little ME.

And I noticed me. As if for the first time.

Perfect
Precious
Curious
Open
Beautiful

CELEBRATING THE TOO MUCH WOMAN

I took a moment to look- to see deeply, to feel, to know, to connect with her essence.

Her eyes are wide.
Her hands poised.
Her mind open.

I was filled with immense love and emotion.
So much so that my eyes welled up and my heart expanded in my chest like a balloon.

I find I am holding my breath for her.

And in that breath, the possibility for her life pauses-

a freezeframe - as the energy of her spirit, which -while alive in me- has been muted, begins to stir.

"Remember me." She whispers.

My body is covered in chills. My angels close in. I lean in to listen.

"Remember me." She says again. And nothing more. So I sit with her. And hold her. And feel her softness. Her trust. Her peace.

And I notice. The way she rises and falls with her sweet breath. The way she relaxes into me. The way her small body fits perfectly in mine. The way our cells merge and the lines blur and suddenly she is no longer outside of me at all.

And I exhale. I will remember you, Darling. I will honour you today.

Don't Dim Any Longer For Their Comfort

Warning.

There is a dangerous woman in your midst.
A woman in love.

She's fallen head over heels for that reflection in the mirror.

With that impish smile,
With the wrinkle in her brow,
With that too loud laugh,
With her Too Much intensity, her Too Much passion, her Too Much sensitivity.

All the Too Muchness of her vulnerability, her wit, her awkwardness, her sass, and yes– even with those thighs.

She is committed to herself.
Ohhh, be careful with this one.

She's unapologetic, self-compassionate and self-forgiving.

She believes deeply in her value and knows she has something important to share with the world.

Celebrating the TOO MUCH WOMAN

She won't dim herself any longer for your comfort...

And, she's really not sorry about it either (gasp).

Careful now, careful.
This one is powerful.

She won't be tamed.
She won't be manipulated.
She won't be used.
And she won't hold back any longer.

She stands on the shoulders of thousands, united by a force from the past and a vision for the future.

Scary huh?
Don't say I didn't warn ya.

Run Your Own Race

I want to go back.

To strip down to my barest essentials.
To the me I really am.
To the me I always was before I dressed up in their expectations.

I want to figure out where I Begin and where the woman the world wants me to be Ends.

I want to trace my steps back to the Starting Line and Get Into Position.

I don't mind that the race has already started and there are others in the lead.

I'm running my Own race.
In my Own lane.
On my Own time.
Forging my Own path now.

And it will take me away sometimes.
Away from the pre-set trail they marked for me.

My intuition will call me into the forest or to the left or through an unpaved grassy field.

Celebrating the TOO MUCH WOMAN

No clear destination but my heart will know the way.

I want to keep running and shed all the hurt and pain and unworthiness as I go.

All the stuff that made me sick and angry and scared.

I will keep running.

Keep moving.
Keep focused.
Keep laughing.
Keep loving.
Keep reminding myself that I am running my Own race.

So I don't come to The End of My life and realize I never even knew myself.

I am Sacred.
I am Divine.
I am Magic.
I am the champion of my own life.
And so are you.

I Love You Anyway

"Shame on you!"

That phrase is right up there with the top cruellest things to say to someone.

Shame is the silent killer in our society.

It's the under-dog that doesn't get enough attention.

The unusual suspect that gets away with unbelievable abominations.

We are all ashamed of something.

Whether legit or imagined – we all have a part of us that we are deathly afraid of exposing.

Shame is a sly cross-dresser masquerading as...

Fear
Cruelty
Sadness
Depression
Bullying
Substance abuse
Cheating

Celebrating the TOO MUCH WOMAN

Obesity
Grief
Abuse
Addiction
Rage

And the list goes on.

As Brene Brown teaches us, "shame corrodes the belief that we are capable of change"... and so we remain the same.

The only antidote to shame is truth and compassion.

While I can't stand for your truth, I can actively love you anyway.

So I speak to the heart of each of you today who, consciously or unconsciously feel unworthy, unlovable, ashamed.

I speak directly to your not-enoughness.

Hear me when I say: Baby, I love you anyway.

Speak Your Truth

Why I speak...

For much of my life, I've been thirsty. So thirsty. Parched.

My mouth dry from speaking untruths and half truths and more than that, from being wide open and not speaking at all.

I imagine my Inner Being brittle and parched like a desert. A barren landscape where nothing much can survive for lack of life sustaining water.

I'd pour myself glass after glass of it. That clear stuff running from the tap.
It would touch my lips and run down my throat and I'd be momentarily relieved.

And yet – moments later – my tongue, searching desperately for more liquid gold, would swell again wanting more.

"Why can't I get enough?" I would ask. "When will this craving end? Why can nothing fill this empty crevice of desire? How cruel a Universe to plant a desperate yearning in me that can get no relief?"

I'd drop into a deep bath and let the water drown me. Perhaps by osmosis my body will absorb what it needs from the outside in?

I'd wait. Holding my breath. Nothing.

How is it that I can swim in a pool of answers and none will match my question?

I was so thirsty. Looking outside me for anything to quench this unrelenting thirst.

The tears of surrender start to flow. Squeezing the last precious ounces of moisture from my body.
Surely this is the end.

I licked my upper lip where a salty tear has pooled and come to rest. It tasted of me.
My sadness. My joy. My success and failure. My truth and my lies. Me.

That drop. That one drop tasted good.

It came from me. Deep within and as me as my DNA. It is all of me and it is true.

And as more tears fall, I let them slide into my mouth and replenish me. Drop after drop.
Truth.
Truth.Truth.

I am a fountain. It is all within me.
Every ounce of nourishment springing up from the depths of my Spirit.

It is life-affirming and honest and is the only thing that will save me.

I am a fountain. And as I turn on the faucet of my Truth, the water of life begins to flow.

This is why I speak. The truth gives life to my soul.

I invite you to speak yours.

You Inspire Me

I have watched you from a distance.
Your quiet determination.
Your soft, cleansing tears.
Your resolve to stand back up.

I am with you.

Standing one step behind, yet always within arm's reach so that when it gets really tough, you will feel my steady hand on your shoulder.

I am in awe of you.

You inspire resilience in me.
A tenacity I didn't know I had.

Not by your strength or as a result of your perfection.

No.

But by your courage to get the hell back up.
Over and over,
Time and again.

Your never-giving-up-ness dares me to peel myself out of bed every day.

Celebrating the TOO MUCH WOMAN

Even when my bones ache with the weariness of the world.

To write and dream and bare my soul.
Because sometimes you matter to me more than I do.

Thank you,
Thank you,
Thank each of you.

You lift me up. Every damn day.

What's It Gonna Take For You?

"What's it gonna take?"

I'm charged with these words often.

When my life feels out of alignment. When there is a death. When I lose something I love.

When the four corners of my Blanket of Comfort have me tucked in a stranglehold, and I mistake Routine and Familiarity for happiness and peace.

"What's it gonna take, Gina?"

What helps me most is visiting the bedside of my Future Self.

She lays there in a white cotton gown, silver hair floating like a shimmering crown around her wise face, a knowing smile, she reaches her hand out to me.

She doesn't have to speak. Her eyes are words. They tell the story of possibility and regret.

They talk to me with both great urgency and unconditional love.

Her eyes know how to touch me and move me.

They know exactly what to say.

So today I begin Day One...again.

Refocusing on my mission and daring to Play Bigger.

Taking chances with my voice, my heart and trusting the path.

Knowing I am guided and this work is important.

But before I go, one question for you.

What's it gonna take, Darling?

I'm Not Here For Anyone Else

I could be doing a million things.

I should be doing a million things.

I seriously have a million things to do.

So I'm taking a bath.

Because it's the only thing I WANT to do.

This is a new space for me.

To luxuriate in pure Desire.

To self-indulge in Bliss.

To bathe comfortably in my needs and allow the hungry outstretched hands of the world to dissipate in my mind.

Voices in my head tell me I'm here to be of service, to give, to love, to shed light, to help heal, to teach and to never, ever stop.

They are relentless.
They are loud.
And they are Wrong.

Celebrating the TOO MUCH WOMAN

I am not here for anyone else.
I am not a saviour.
I am not the answer.

I am here to be true to myself.

To live honestly and in integrity.

To be clear about where I begin and where I end.

To be a Light–not for the sake of others–but because it is Who I Am at my core.

I've been trying so hard, too hard, to BE SOMETHING for the world, for my kids and for you.

The pressure has me drowning.

And like the bubbles I am bathed in, the moment I try to grab at That Thing, it pops beneath the pressure of my desperate Intention.

What if all I needed to do was Be Me?

Take excellent care of me.
Love me.
Attend to me.
Be accountable to me.
Heal me.
Be honest and faithful to me.

What if everything I hope to gift to you really began with me?

Then we could each be responsible for our own happiness and meet somewhere in the middle.

Carefree.
Whole.

Independent.
Full of love.

I'm not sure this will work.

As a former journalist, I'm honestly more in love with the questions themselves.

I know it's not popular to say "Me First" in a world where servitude and martyrdom are glorified.

But what many of us know, having lived life on bloody, bended knees, is that the best offering we have, comes from a place of joy, rest and a full spirit.

But I'm pruning now so I'll just leave this right here.

Let's Just Love Each Other

You Are Not Broken. I refuse to see you this way.

I won't accept that there is anything wrong with you, nor will I believe you *need* my help.

This broken paradigm has sucked us all down the drain of personal development.

Selling us a myth that we are Less Than. That we require the help of experts to fix our broken bits.

I stand for a revolutionary new approach.

I stand for a truth that declares that Your Path, Your Experiences and Your Spirit have paved the way for your Inner Wisdom to emerge.

Within you are all the ingredients you need to create the masterpiece that is your life.

All you need are the tools to access and trust this inner knowing.

All you need is faith – mine and yours – in your innate ability to stand fully in your truth and handle your shit.

Let's stop trying to fix each other.

Gina Hatzis

Let's stop trying to save each other.

Instead, let's just love one other.

Let's bear witness to one another.

Let's set an intention to truly See one another.

Let's be a mirror to reflect the beauty and grace and strength in one another.

Let's bless each other.

Let's hold each other.

And honour each other AS WE ARE.

Because invisibility is what suffocates the soul

And then, maybe each one of us will have the courage and the freaking audacity to stand be seen in All Our Glory.

Stop Dodging Your Glory

I was in conversation with a friend today about things gone wrong. What hadn't worked, mistakes made and opportunities missed.

I couldn't help but swoop in to point out all of the accomplishments and markers of success she'd had.

And it got me wondering–what is it about the human psyche that has us dodging our glory?

What is it about Me that has me working so hard to rise to an occasion, only to allow the pinnacle moment to last the length of a sneeze before it's–on to the Next?

Today I choose to reflect on my success. I celebrate how, despite having an emotionally turbulent year, I refused to abandon myself.

I stayed committed to sitting with the discomfort,
to giving myself sleep when I needed it,
escape when it was warranted,
creative expression when it bubbled up
and forgiveness when it didn't.

I'm proud of being a little more honest and a little less pleasing.

I'm proud of saying Goodbye when it was necessary and No when it was hard.

I'm proud of letting people down in order to honour my soul and I'm proud of forgiving myself when the one I let down was Me.

I'm proud that I screwed up.

And I'm proud I made some messes. Because it means I took a chance and I survived the wreckage.

I'm proud of big risks and scary leaps of faith.

I'm proud of my growth and also proud of my awareness that in some ways, I haven't grown one bit.

I'm proud most of all that I stayed in the ring.
Maskless, naked, bloody, weary.
Tears streaming, head back, laughing, arms open, heart full, breathing deeply.

Your turn.

Let's Focus On Our Brilliance Today

Let's get really clear today about what's important.

The 'Stuff of Life' kind of important.

Let's agree not to get bogged down in the pettiness of life – the details, the minutiae, the weeds.

Let's rise above the need to Be Right, the need to Get It All done, the need to Feel Superior, the need to Be Perfect, the need to Have All the Answers.

Just for today, let's focus on how powerful we are when we express love, when we listen intently, when we smile, when we take pause and breathe in the moment.

Let's own our brilliance and share it generously with no exception or conditions or limits.

Just for today, let's don the best version of ourselves and flaunt our beauty and joy proudly so that anyone we come in contact with leaves us wondering, "Wow...I feel amazing. What just happened?"

Just For Today, let's all tap into our Highest, most Graceful and Loving selves and do the work of our Souls.

Just for today, let's take some time to centre ourselves in our own energy, fill our souls with love and Source energy, hope and inspiration.

And then, instead of focusing on the ripple of our thighs, create a ripple of Goodness so powerful, it bathes every corner of the globe in our Light.

Who's with me?

The Waiting Is The Most Important Part

(Warning: The following musings may cause reflection, deep thought and a few minutes of time. Consult your heart and watch before reading.)

I'm in the Waiting.

The Waiting is that space after pain or suffering or a major shake-up in your life where you have found your breath again, and the spinning has slowed.

The Waiting is a place where a settling of sorts happens.

Not of dust settling – no...but shards of glass and other sharp objects like old belief systems and wake up calls and hard edges of comfort zones.

The Waiting aches.

A space when the old no longer fits over your thighs and the swell of your soul.

A space where the new has not yet arrived to provide direction and solace and hope.

The Waiting is limbo.

Like the party game with a stick where you constantly challenge yourself to bend backward to make it safely under your Truth and out the other side.

Over and over you go. The limbo stick lowers once again and you wonder how far back you can bend without breaking or collapsing.

Sometimes you surprise yourself and make it.
Other times you fall back.

No matter...the music still plays and the game continues.

The Waiting is the most important part of your awakening.

It is tender and raw and pregnant with possibility.

A place were any choice exists for you if you can just hang in there.

The Waiting is there to develop the most important muscle in your body.

Your Trust Muscle.

This muscle will serve you, sustain you, save you.

If you are in the Waiting, time messes with you.

Just as in any waiting room, minutes can feel like hours, days even..and you wonder how long you can just sit and wait for your name to be called – to rescue you from here.

If you are in the Waiting Room, it feels very lonely.

You know there are other people waiting too but no one can understand YOUR anxiety, your situation, your pain.

So you all sit together avoiding eye contact and staring down at your folded hands, in your perceived aloneness.

But I dare you to look up. To look left and look right at those around you.

Look up and see me. I'm sitting here too. Let's hang on together – grab my hand. We will wait.

And trust.

Together.

And believe that it will all be worth the Wait.

When Truth Has Legs

It's such a beautiful experiment, this weeding out of my tribe.

Speak your truth and they'll scatter like cockroaches crisped by the light.

I don't blame them, really. Heck, sometimes I wanna run from it too.

The truth is the devil you don't know.

It has red eyes and peeks through your closet door where skeletons of lies hang shamefully, lifelessly, pitifully.

Truth's hot breath is all it takes to rattle those bones and scare off the faint of heart.

But when confronted by That Moment...

The one that has my heart ripping the delicate skin from my chest...

The Moment where my heart says Fight and my Mind says Flee...

The Moment that has me split in two at the crossroads of Truth and Lies...

Celebrating the TOO MUCH WOMAN

I pause.

I gather All of Me – Past, Present and Future, and we throw our hands in the middle of the circle.

I zoom out and for a split second, I see the whole picture, the one that is my life.

And my Spirit holds her breath, the whole world does, awaiting my decision.

And the calm Knowing blankets me.

I am not Nothing.

My truth has legs. And it will Stand.

It may be uncomfortably ugly, bizarre and ungodly. It make seem non-sensical and pathetic. It may be the opposite of your truth. It may make your Truth quiver in a cloak of self-consciousness.

But no matter.

My truth has legs. And it will Stand

Surrender and Accept the Journey

This has been such a pivotal year of growth for me in many areas of my life.

And as much as I'm a proponent of the Evolution of the Soul, I don't remember consciously asking for ALL of my major life lessons to hit me like a cyclone in a span of 18 months.

As I've birthed these new parts of me, the labour pains have forced me to confront all of the spiritual lessons I understood and have been taught 'in theory' for the past 20 years...and test the shit out of them. One by one.

So yeah, it's been a roller coaster, (Ha...understatement).

And I haven't quite decided how I feel about it all...but ya know what else?

Despite the sharp turns, sharp pains and sharp lessons, I have never felt more loved.

Never.

The Universe has gifted me with a tribe of loving Souls who remind me daily Why it's Worth it and Who I am being called to Be.

I find that my heart is very tender, and my body is asking to be touched as if it were a newborn baby. With gentle, adoring love.

While embodying a Wild Woman Warrior exterior to manage the assaults of a conflicted consciousness in transition, just beneath my armour I am so tender and delicate.

I am healing ancient wounds of many lifetimes, for many ancestors and on behalf of many sisters.

I surrender and accept this journey willingly.

Even when surrender and acceptance has my jaw clenched and seizes my heart, the Love and Kindness I am nestled in gives me the courage to Breathe Through each contraction.

I dare not sugar coat this process...for anyone traveling the Dark Night of the Soul it is not a path to tread upon lightly.

Sometimes I trot, like a freaking multi-coloured unicorn and at other times I crawl scraping dirt with my fingernails.

But always, always, always with your Love,
I Move Forward.

Thank you.
I am eternally grateful.

What If the Detour Is the Path?

I'm on a crazy detour in my life.

I'm off-roading, bigtime.

To be honest, it's an unexpected ride that's got me white-knuckling the steering wheel while I cry-scream-laugh over every bump and turn.

Part of me is craving the smooth, cement trail of predictability and calm, while my Spirit is alive with the rush of possibility and adventure of the unknown.

Questions flood my mind.

Have I veered to far from the path?
Will I ever find my way back?
What if I'm making a terrible mistake?
Is this GPS even freaking working?

And then...Oh la la!

The Highest, Wisest part of me asks the question du jour:

What if this crazy, messed-up, train-wreck of a detour IS THE PATH?

What if this place where I believed I was lost was actually en route to my sweet destiny?

That would mean, my GPS is, in fact, working!

And I am...we are...PRECISELY where we are supposed to be in this moment.

What if this space, while uncomfortable, unfamiliar (and frankly unappealing), is all part of a Divine plan to get you to the Place you need to be?

What if where you are is the EXACT pivot point to shift the trajectory of your journey and land you in precisely in the space you need to be with the awareness and wisdom you crave?

What if this is all perfect and we just can't see the light around the bend?

What if the detour IS the path?

Well now...

That changes everything doesn't it?

Making Friends With Fear

I want your undivided attention. I want to speak to the Heart of you.

I want to speak to those who tell me the #1 thing holding you back from living the life you desire is Fear.

Yeah, no kidding.

A close friend of mine asked me yesterday where I got the courage to live so Fearlessly and speak so powerfully.

I smiled.

Gina Hatzis

It's so funny to me that I am perceived as Fearless. I dance with Fear Every. Damn. Day.

Fear nudges me awake in the morning, reminding me to start worrying because I have so much on my plate.

It creeps up my neck and stiffens it – like a death hold – reminding me of the pain of leaving my comfort zone.

Fear interrupts my breath the moment I sit down, take a break or when I'm having fun, reminding me that the clock is tick, tick ticking away and I don't deserve any respite.

Fear shoots down my arms and numbs my fingers as I hit the Post button, reminding me of my precious vulnerability.

Fear washes over me as I stand in front of my audience before a talk, telling me that I have nothing of value to say.

Fear grips my heart the moment my head it hits the pillow, reminding me that it is relentless in its chase, and like the Boogeyman, will never, ever let me rest.

I have never been Fearless. And I don't think I ever will be. In fact, I'm not sure I ever s*hould* be.

See, I look at Fear differently now.

Having been scared out of my mind, and still choosing to move in the direction of my heart's desire, I can see something different from the other side. I see Fear for what it really is.

Like the Wizard of Oz, it is hardly the big, imposing, omnipotent monster of my worst nightmares. I have seen behind the curtain of Fear and have sighed with relief and compassion.

See Fear is the littlest part of me. It is my precious 2 year-old self, afraid of my own Greatness, which I mistook in the shadows as a big, hairy monster.

Fear is the Big Wagging Finger shaming me for my Too Much-ness.

But Darling, my fear loves me. And your Fear loves you.

It is just misdirecting its Love, much like a fearful parent. It thinks it's protecting you from this horrible possibility. When in fact, it's keeping you from the very thing you want most.

I have made friends with Fear, in my own way.
I smile when it shows up baring its sharp, gleaming teeth.

I look it right in the eyes and softly whisper, "Thank you, Darling. I know what you're trying to do. But, I've got this. It's all gonna be okay".

Fear often looks back, quizzically and sometimes it roars even louder.

But I have learned to stand firm, with love and confidence, in the knowing that
I've Got This.

And, my friend, so do you.

What A Too Much Woman Doesn't Do

Not too long ago, I had my first boudoir shoot.

I always said I'd do it "when"…Ya know the deal.

Two short years ago I would NEVER have posted this…ever, ever. For shame!
I'm a freaking professional, a public figure, a mother!

But I am nothing, NOTHING if not a woman who walks my talk.

A Too Much Woman doesn't say, "But my thighs, my chin, my arms…"

A Too Much Woman isn't striving for perfection.

She knows her worth is inherent.

A Too Much Woman doesn't shrink from life.
She expands into possibility.

A Too Much Woman doesn't wait for Some Day.
She owns the moment.

A Too Much Woman doesn't dim in shame.
She shines in her full glory.

Celebrating the TOO MUCH WOMAN

A Too Much Woman won't shrink from fear.
She rises with courage.

A Too Much Woman refuses to tuck her juiciness away.
She is radiant in her Divine essence.

I'm a Too Much Woman...and I'm dangerous, can't you see?

Call In The Magic

From my interview with New York Times best-selling author Pam Grout of *E-Squared*, I learned to "Call in the Magic".

So when I'm seeking a little something extra from the Universe to support me, I simply ask.

This is the kind of magic I experience when I do:

After meditating on a big decision yesterday, I was a LITTLE nervous.

So I asked, "Oh Universe! Sweet Divine Guidance...This is a mighty big one. I'm shakin' in my boots!

And although my intuition is clear, I would love a Big Sign. (I'm talking an unmistakable, absolutely undeniable, there's-no-way-this-could-be-a-mistake kinda sign) that I'm on the right track.

I wanna know that I'm moving in the right direction and I will be fully supported. Thank you!"

I sat for a few moments...waiting, and heard a Canadian Goose honk in the distance.

I chuckled to myself. "OK, cute Universe. But I need a louder, more obvious sign than just a little honk."

Celebrating the TOO MUCH WOMAN

A few hours later, I was driving home at sunset and was shaken by the sound of a dozen or so Canada Geese flying right above my car. They were SO unbelievably loud that I heard them over the radio blasting!

They were flying so low and honking so loudly I was actually startled.

Not only by the sheer volume of their honks, but by the oh-so-obvious sign from the Universe.

"Did you say a louder, more obvious sign?" She chided me.

Haha, yes, yes I did.

Message received Loud and Clear.

What magic will you call in today?

When Roots Go Deep

My Roots go deep.

Beyond my legs and past my toes
My Roots go deep.

They spring like lightning bolts into the Grand Mother of Earth
Past soil and sand and rock.

My Roots zip past the Centre and go beyond Space and Time
Swirling around my ancestors, dancing in their struggle and courage, their joy and pain.

My Roots go deep
Shooting beyond lifetimes and lifelines and into the infinite abyss.

Back to Source
Back to Origin
Back to the Beginning

My Roots go so deep they stretch into the future
Breathing life and resilience and hope into my lineage, yet unborn.

Celebrating the TOO MUCH WOMAN

I have no fear.
The wind can moan and scream and threaten all it wants.
It can taunt and tease and torment all day, all night, all over me.

But I have no fear.
None.
Because, my Roots.
They go Deep.

Bring the Light, Be The Sun

I Forget sometimes who I am and the Power that I yield...

The Power of my Light.

I shuffle around in a dark room
Grasping
Groping
Bumping into things
Moaning
Groaning
Blaming
Resenting
Lamenting

Where is that damn light? And why is it so dark in here anyway?

I forget that a power station doesn't find energy or receive energy...It generates it.

The sun doesn't reflect light or plug into light...It creates it.

I am that powerful. And, sweet friend, so are you.

Today, when it's so easy to commiserate in the dark

Today, when the world feels heavy and the collective moan is one of despair and hopelessness.

Today, as we feel the ache for humanity and righteousness deep in our bones

Won't you Be the Light?

Bring it. Rock it.

Let it shine so bright people are drawn to you like moths to a flame.
And stand in awe of the brightness you exude.

And as they lean closer in wonder of you, they catch a spark of your light and suddenly they become Light themselves.

And before you know it, the ripple of your light has created a wildfire!
And it lights up the sky. And it's glorious!

You can do that. Yes. You can do that.

Bring the Light, Baby. You are the sun.

Truth Is Gonna Find You

Truth.
It's gonna find you.

It knows where you live, all your hiding places, and the dark secret crevices of your mind, where you try to escape to.

Just try to shrug it off, tuck it down, sleep it away.

See if the silent treatment keeps Truth in its place.

Or if the Don't-you-dare-Mother-of-all-death stares across the room can keep it in check.

Be busy. Be nice. Be a bitch. Be successful. Be sexy. Be thin. Be perfect. Be a chirpy mom, a badass boss, a kick-butt entrepreneur, a selfie slayer.

Be whatever you want, but Truth is gonna find you.

Hide behind the smile, the latte, the 2 kids, 3 cats, the 4 hours sleep, the 5 km run-for-a-cure, (*Aren't you something?*).

Hide behind the crazy schedule, the filters, the weight loss, the fantastic vacay pics (*Wish you were here*), the girls night out, the degree, the recycled memes and all that "love and light".

Go on. Give it your best shot.

Celebrating the TOO MUCH WOMAN

See how far you can run, get a head start, take months, years if you dare.

But Truth – it's gonna find you.

It cares not about convenience or convention, or age, schedules, hot flashes or how ready you feel.

Truth is not interested in the seasons and how busy you are at work; how guilty you feel and what other people will say.

Truth wants only one thing.

To be acknowledged.

And it will stop at nothing.

It will haunt your sheets at night, messing with your dreams and REM sleep.

It will creep into your cells, scramble the circuits and present as illness, pain, swelling, throbbing, numbness and muffin-top.

It will rattle your emotions like the bones of the skeleton you have tucked in the back of your soul's closet.

But Truth. It's a relentless Mo-Fo.
And it's coming for you.

Because, Baby, you deserve it.

Two Stories About Why This Is Happening

I recently received a rude awakening.

A long-standing challenge I believed I had 'gotten over' came back to bite me in the you-know-where.

The bite hurt my pride – yes. (*I'm here...again?*)

But more than that, it rocked my Ego that has this perfectly crafted story about "how far I've come" and "how hard I've worked" and why "I deserve to be over this" by now.

We all have this story.
But there is another one.

I want to suggest that your life has two stories that run in parallel.

The first story is directed by your Ego, and the starring roles are played by Impatience, Worry, Entitlement, Fear and the Diva Victim.

This narrative follows your hopes and dreams, and celebrates them, when they arrive.

It also quickly becomes resentful, angry and frustrated when they don't.

In this story, everything neatly falls into two categories: Positive and Negative...all according to our Ego's opinion of what is Supposed to happen, how and when.

But there is another story.

This story is directed by your Soul.

The key actors are Wisdom, Growth, Compassion and Truth.

This narrative doesn't judge events as good or bad, right or wrong, wins and losses.

This script is merely interested in your Soul's journey and in the depth and breadth of lessons learned. This narrative invites you to wrestle with core questions and gain greater understanding.

It wants you to dive deeper and soar higher than the acute meaning of this failure, this pain, this loss, this frustration.

I am currently faced with decisions to play Bigger than ever and face some monstrous Fears.

This has forced me to go deeper and wrestle with questions about life's purpose versus mothering, service versus self-care, financial success versus joy and play.

When I focus on the story directed by the Ego, it says this is the moment I've been waiting for and it better all play out exactly as planned because I deserve this!

When I refocus on this story through the lens of my Soul, I recognize that these issues are the ones I have been avoiding all along and are main themes I'm meant to wrestle through in this lifetime.

We all have these two stories playing simultaneously.

The Ego's story is a painful rendition of what is happening and why it should be otherwise.

If I look at the same situation through the Soul's directorial lens, I take myself out of the shallow story of what Should be happening, and I am invited to receive the rich lessons I am here to learn.

Only through this story can I begin to evolve into the whole person I am intended to be.

And so, it is with you.

How to start looking at your life through your Soul's perspective?

Start by asking, "What does this experience have to do with what my Soul is here to learn?"

Take Up Space

I wrote an Ode to my Thighs today.

To the part of me I have never loved, always rejected.

I think thighs are one of the sexiest and most powerful parts of a woman's body.

Soft, vulnerable. A gateway. A runway.

They say yes or no. They are discreet or provocative. They leave space or block it.

Strong, sturdy. No bullshit.
(Sigh)... I love thighs.
How could I not love my own?

But this isn't a post about thighs.

It's about ownership. It's about being seen. It's about shining.

It's about Space.

And taking it. Filling it. Owning it.

Shunning parts of our self, whether physical or otherwise, is a license to shrink.

Gina Hatzis

The inward compression of a Soul. The concave collapse of a Spirit.

Where the heart gasps for air beneath the weight of shame and apology.

Hiding or masking any part of ourselves is denying all of ourselves.

And I intend to stop.

I intend to TAKE UP SPACE.

Stand taller.
Be big.
Ask for More.
Get loud.
Open your freaking mouth.
Show your teeth.
Lick your lips.
Boldly stare.
Don't flinch.
Reach out your arms.
Wider.
Open your hands.
Ask. Ask again.
Pause.
Don't fill the space with weakness.
Or shame. Or second guessing.
Heart open.
Receive. More.
Lungs full.
Legs rooted.
Knees locked.
Feet planted.

Celebrating the TOO MUCH WOMAN

Roar. Purr. Cry. Snort. Yell. Whimper.
Drop down.
Roll around.
Make a mess.
Make art.
Make love.
Make mistakes.
Make anything.

Just Take Up Space.

Take Up Space.

Darling, Take Up Space

A Beautiful Mess

"She is delightfully chaotic. A beautiful mess.

Loving her is a splendid pleasure." –Steve Maraboli

It's wonderful to be in a space where I'm unapologetic about my beautiful mess.
This delightful chaos is MINE.
I own it.
Gone are the days I would measure worthiness by who's loving me and how much.
I can hardly believe I'm typing this.
Tears of grace and relief and honestly tumble from pools of my deep Truth.
After a lifetime (maybe many), of chasing the shadow of my value in the gaze of Another, I am standing firmly in Warrior Pose: feet planted, thighs tight, spine strong, chest proud, shoulders squared, eyes daring, heart dancing.
I am a supreme gift. An adventure. An uncompromising lover. A dreamer. A wild flower. A raging bull. A drama queen. And a beautiful, scribbled mess.
And I am still worth the trouble.
Every bit of it.
In fact, I'm a rare treasure.
An enigma. A mirage. A dream.
And Baby, so are you.

Choosing To Be Chocolate

If you're looking, you can find me in my blanket fort...

I'm amidst a storm of Busy-ness, preparing for a tsunami to hit.

Oh, the thrill!
The excitement!
The opportunity!
The pressure to Get It Right.

For a recovering perfectionist like me, having a once-in-a-lifetime opportunity knock at my door is akin to dropping a recovering alcoholic right in the middle of a Spring Break Rave.

I watch the clock tick tick ticking down – a bomb about to detonate – and feel the Hands of Time grip my soul and begin to squeeze the joy out of my Spirit.

My essential self oozes through clenched fingers as the pressure to Be and Become and Achieve once the clock strikes midnight, displaces my peace and inner harmony.

I feel like a kid in the dark during a game of Hide-and-Seek. My heart palpitates. My hands sweaty.

Gina Hatzis

Will I be found, or found out?

I don't wanna play.

The tension isn't joyful for me.
It feels like pressure.

I want Peace.
Because this is who I am.

I choose to relax like melted chocolate and sweetly drip drip drip into the future.

Licking my lips from the Joy of Self Celebration and Expansion.

Sucking my fingers from the ecstasy of being comfortable in my skin and the perfect imperfection of my being.

That's the energy I choose.

Smooth, sexy and suave like a Latin dancer.

The bachata is my choice.

Relaxed. Intentional. And fully alive.

Time to tuck my superwoman cape back into the drawer of shame and come to terms with the fact that I need help.

That will be my gift to myself. Receiving.

But until then, I'll be hiding in my blanket fort.
If you care to join me knock 3 times...and bring snacks!

Right Where You Are Is The Right Place

"Everyone ends up where they need to be." – Panache Desai

Whether it's a traffic jam, a dead-end relationship, a soul-sucking job or a space of utter confusion...
It's the Right Place.
Because wherever you go, there you are.
The Where is less relevant than the Who.
You could be on a tropical island sipping margaritas and be desperately miserable.
Or you could wake up on a Monday morning marinating in a pool of utter joy for the opportunity to greet the dawn of a new day.
Wherever you are is exactly the place intended for you.
It's where you need to be, to experience this moment.
You are right on schedule.
You are in the right place. At the right time.
Simply because it's where you are.
Stand firm in that space.
Take a look around and own this truth.
This is where I am.
And it's exactly where I need to be in this moment.
Wherever you are, just know you're not alone

You Are A Storm

I'm a storm.
I get waves of inspiration and possibility.
I swell with love and hope.
I burst at the seams with a vision that forces my reptilian brain to poise for Fight or Flight.
Within this passionate reverie, I feel lifted, supported by the angels of my ancestors, their wings guiding me up and out of my comfort zone and fears.
They speak to me in urgent, breathless whispers
To keep moving forward
To not mind the hands, the obstacles, the wind that tries to block my path.
In those moments, I know this dream, this desire, this wish ISN'T ABOUT ME – it isn't even mine.
It is the hope of the Universe.
And it chose me to make it manifest.
And this is true for You.
Whatever is seeded deep in your heart - big, small, radical, ordinary, obvious, irrelevant...
It chose You.
All it requires is for you to say "yes".
Do us all a favour...say yes.
Thank you for saying yes.

Celebrating the TOO MUCH WOMAN

You are more than a body.
You have the strength of the whole Universe within you.
You are a storm with skin.
This is dedicated to some amazing souls moving through some big changes and choosing to play bigger in the world.
I am proud to know each of you and to have you be part of my storm.

Your Soul Contract

I have a soul contract in this lifetime.

We all do.
And mine is an agreement to stir things up.

To use my voice, my words, my gift to rattle the bones of comfort, complacency and convention.

I'm not here to link arms and sing Kumbaya.

I'm here to stand for Truth – yours and mine, no matter how unlikable that makes me or how uncomfortable that makes you.

I cannot confuse my mission with an undercurrent of neediness to be accepted and be seen as anything other than who I am.

This confusion taints the power of my intention.

And this is also true for you.

You have a soul contract.

And it cannot be honoured when your energy is distracted by a need to be liked.

The people who stick around when you undress your Truth are the only ones you need.
They are the ones you came for.

Being loved for how you look when you exit the Dressing Room of Approval will never be enough. It will never fill the crevices of your desire. And you will always be left yearning.

Be open to self-awareness. Yes.

Be open to constructive feedback. Absolutely.

Be open to the opportunities to grow and evolve and regroup into your Highest Self. 100%.

Be open to the fact that you have been assigned this contract because you are capable and worthy of its mission.

And Baby, wear your Truth.

I Wanna Be With Those People

More and more and more this is becoming apparent in my life: my skin and soul are permeable.

And the energy I surround myself with penetrates...Deep.

The people I spend the most time with impact me greatly.

They have the potential to influence my thoughts, trigger my wounds, elevate my vision or gut my dreams.

I wanna be around people who Get It.

I wanna surround myself with the Dreamers, the Lovers, the Artists, the Way-showers, the Do-Gooders, the Trail Blazers.

Those unafraid to take chances.

Those willing to grow and be uncomfortable.

Those insisting on taking responsibility for their lives.

Those who let love lead the way.

Those that see vulnerability as strength.

Those who think beyond the moment.

Celebrating the TOO MUCH WOMAN

Those who believe in impossible shit.

Those who take ridiculous chances.

Those whose presence emanates peace.

Those I can feel safe enough around to show up as myself.

Those with pure intentions.

Those who energize rather than deplete me.

Those who see Possibility as their primary driver and Love as the vehicle.

Those who focus on the stars on a dark night and dance wildly in the light of the moon.

Those who cry hard and loud and laugh like a crazy hyena.

Those people.

They Get It.

How I Love This Body

This body could not be more ready for the beach.

Not because it's buff and fit.
Not because it's in its prime.
And surely not because I've earned it through dedicated focus and endless workouts.

No, simply because this body was Made for the beach.

It's my happy place.
Where I escape to in my mind's eye to find solace in the midst of a hectic day.

What crawling belly-down through the dark night of the soul has taught me, is how truly devoted this body is to me.

I have ignored it, starved it, shunned it, dimmed it, cursed it, stuffed it, booty-camped it and deprived it.

And it has stuck right by me like faithful Old Yeller.

And it has earned my respect and deep Reverence by not giving up on me.

I have deep love for every soft curve and robust bend.

I am in love with her supple sensuality and TooMuch audacity.

Celebrating the TOO MUCH WOMAN

I treasure her Herculean strength and unparalled resilience.

The way she speaks to me in tongues, sending me love messages in a secret language that only I can understand...sighhhh.

How she wakes me up every day without fail! Every single day for 43 years!
Talk about loyalty.

Oh, I love this body.
And she deserves the freaking beach.
Doesn't yours?

The Winner Is The One Who Finds Herself

We spend the first part of our lives becoming what the world tells us to become.

And Then.

There is this moment, this wave, this tug, this whisper, this unsettling...

When we look at ourselves in the mirror.

When we become sweaty underneath the layers of false identity.

When someone calls our name and it feels odd to respond.

When even our nakedness feels like a mask.

And we ask:

What happened?
Where am I?
Who am I?

OH, HELL NO!

And the Brave Ones don't shy from the reflection in the looking glass.

They stare back – eyes brimming with Compassion and Desire, Curiosity and Defiance.

And then the UNBECOMING begins.

STRIP IT ALL OFF, LOVES.

Retrace your steps back to the starting line.

The race is of no consequence now.
The finish line isn't on the other side of the masquerade.

The winner is the one who finds herself.

And knows herself.
And dances naked in her glory.

The Mighty Roar

I am One.
And I am powerful as One.

I have a mighty roar.
A defiant step.
A loving heart.
A clear intention.
And resilience oozing from my cells.

And yet, to walk this path with a tribe just as Mighty, as Defiant, as Loving, as Clear and as Resilient, is like walking with a pack of Lions.

Untouchable.
Aligned.
Fully Supported.
Unmatched.

This is the secret sauce.

I am so grateful to have found mine. Thank you for being here.

ROAAR!

I Believe in All These Things

> "**Even if I knew tomorrow that the world would go to pieces, I would still plant my apple tree.**"
> –Dr. Martin Luther King

I may be resilient.
Or simply a stubborn mule.
But I won't lose my faith in humanity.

As a once-upon-a-time journalist, I tasted hopelessness...reporting on story after story that left me cold and sad and sick.

I spent my days stitching together the seams of tragedy and despair and trying to make sense of crazy.

At some point I wondered, "Who am I really serving, anyway?" and to what end?

It wasn't until I left that industry and began to shift the focus of my energy towards peace and possibility that I felt a resurgence of hope.

I discovered inspiring people forging new pathways of love and lifting the world with their generosity and gifts.

I noticed random good deeds and witnessed the kindness of strangers.

I found, for every story that made my heart ache, there was one the made it swell with joy.

Oh look, I'm not blind. I see the crazy going on.

It's everywhere. If you choose to look for it.

But lose hope?
Throw in the towel?
There's no passion in that.

I believe in burning and longing and hanging on by your finger nails.

I believe in holding on to the sliver of a chance my team has before the buzzer dings.

I believe in fat chances and the odds of pigs flying.

I will believe in Heaven even if we don't have a hope in Hell.

I have seen too much Good to succumb to the dark side.

And even if I knew it would all go to pieces...
I would still plant my apple tree.

Live The Well-Lived Life

"Teach her the Magic is inside of her, not out there."

"Ah yes!" my heart says. "Absolutely!"

And yet, how can we teach what we don't live?

My SUPREME duty is to heal myself, love myself, grow myself, dote on myself, nurture myself, stretch myself, trust myself, respect myself, honour myself and take exceptional care of myself.

All love grows from the magic within.

It's not out there.

How DARE I ask my child to believe what I don't model?

What AUDACITY to ask her to honour the magic within when I myself keep looking elsewhere?

What LUNACY to encourage her to chase her dream while I tiptoe around mine?

The best gift I can give my child is the example of a life well-lived...

Passionate. Limitless. Abundant.

That is how I shall love her.

Through loving myself.

Your Own Soulmate

> "Sometimes your soulmate is yourself.
> Sometimes you have to be the love of your life
> until you discover that type of love in someone else."
> –R H Sin

I love this thought.

I love this without apology to the romantics, the Hollywood movies and those searching earnestly for their "twin flame".

I love knowing that even without Seeking and Giving and damn,
even without understanding love, that the journey to loving myself IS the cat's meow.

It IS the ultimate Love Affair of my life.

When I'm in a vibration of self-acceptance and self-compassion and self-awareness...

EVERYTHING in my external world becomes dewy and sparkly and yes, unicorns gallop by farting rainbows. (You should see them!)

Remember falling head over heels in love?

Celebrating the TOO MUCH WOMAN

When you don't walk, but float?

When you don't talk, but sing?

When you don't even want to eat or sleep or watch mindless t.v. or complain or gossip or lament?

When you're in a fog of La-La-Land and everywhere you go birds are singing your song, traffic is parting and you wear that dopey perma-grin on your face?

That feeling is your birthright, Darling.

That state of mind is an inside job and if you aren't there, haven't been there or have forgotten how to even get there, that is job #1.

If you're waiting for someone else to fill you, raise you up or complete you, Darling, see a doctor, because you are suffering from amnesia!
You have forgotten that...you. are. whole.

Be your own soulmate.

And, for goodness sake, not tomorrow, or on the weekend or when you drop the weight or get the guy.

Tick tock. Tick tock. That's your time slipping away.

Stop planning your Netflix marathon tonight or your weeks' vacation.

Start crafting the love affair of your life and

Get
to
The
Business
Of

GINA HATZIS

Being
Your
Own
Soul
Mate

Stop waiting. Don't treat today like the boyfriend you are holding on to until the right guy comes along.

Honour your One Precious Life and take responsibility for your joy.

Today.
Now.

Stop reading this and go love on yourself.
Because no one is gonna love you like you can.

No one.

The Roar

Every day, the Lioness in me becomes bolder.

I feel the ROAR start in my toes, travel up my strong grounded legs and shoot up my solid spine, and into the rumbling in my throat...

"Be Brave!"

I hear the echoes of my lineage chanting from the past...pounding their fists in the air and stomping their feet on the ground ...sending me ripples of courage and fierce love.

All the hairs on my body stand at attention- In Reverence- paying homage to the dreams and desires of The Ancestors.

My heart pounds strong and proud knowing that my Bravery will heal past wounds and prevent future pain.

"Be brave!"

Chant the children of the future yet unborn, who will stand firmly on the dust of my shoulders.

They are reading the chapter of the book I am now writing with my choices and they are coming up to their favourite part ...

Gina Hatzis

The ROAR!

"Here it comes!" They squeal in excitement. This is the moment.

The Lioness stands tall and strong.

She lets the breeze sweep across her body and waits patiently for the pregnant swell of silence to fill the air.

She takes a long, slow deep breath in.

And In Her Time, she unleashes her Voice.

And lets the whole world know
Past
Present
Future
that She is Free.

Step Fully into Your Too Muchness

Too intense.
Too sensitive.
Too emotional.
Too passionate.
Too revealing.
Too driven.
Too sensual.
Too woo-woo.
Too Much Gina.

Well, I've released all of that messaging. Buh bye!

The Universe would never ask me (or you) to be anything less than what we are.

We are crafted in perfection.

Being authentic is our Birth right.

Step Fully Into You.
The world will adjust.
Or not.

My job is not to tone down to meet the world's mediocrity, but to dare the world to meet my intensity.

This is the tale of a #TooMuchWoman.

You Can't Dim The Sun

People carelessly say, "Be yourself. Love your body. Shine your light"

But they don't also warn, "Baby, it's a dangerous game."

I'm telling you...

You may be objectified, shunned, envied, harassed, ignored and even abused.

People will repel you, be afraid of you, feel threatened by you.

They will label you, mock you, criticize you and humiliate you.

And I say, Yes. All those things, Yes.

But Darling, honour your sacred heart and Do It Anyway.

Dare to Stand and be Seen In Your Full Glory.

Don't dim the light of your Source Energy.

Find the tribe that will celebrate you, applaud you, encourage you, stretch you, elevate you and revere your Weird.

Even if it's a small crew, even if it's one, even if it's me.

Celebrating the TOO MUCH WOMAN

There is room for you at the Table.

Come sit with me.

I've got snacks.

You're meant to shine, Baby,

Because you just can't dim the sun.

Show Up For You

While it IS wonderful to have that special someone in your life …
Everything is sweeter when love and self-acceptance oozes from you.
Show up for you.
Dote on you.
Make time for you.
Gush about you.
Plan special occasions for you.
Be proud of you.
Create magic for you.
Nourish you.
Buy gifts for you.
Fall in love with you.
Trust me…YOU'RE the one.

The Wings Will Appear

Three Things You'll Never Catch Me Doing:

1. Jump (willingly) from a plane
2. Deep sea dive
3. Enter a bikini contest

Too. Freakin'. Scary.

Now ignore everything I just said.

Because if I've learned anything, it's to "never say never".

And as the years pass, I have come to realize the futility of being held back by fear.

Not too long ago I couldn't have imagined delivering talks to thousands of people, negotiating a world tour or naturally home birthing two babies.

Very. Freakin'. Scary.

And yet, in those moments, the pain of NOT doing that thing was always greater than the discomfort of confronting my fear.

So I shelve my fear...

I allow the shoreline to fade slowly into the sky...

I breathe deep into my bones, past the voice of my Inner Critic, past my Ego, past even my primal need to be loved and accepted...

I arrive in a space where there is a strange Calm, a Knowingness that this is the next right step for me.

All of my cells stand at attention and I'm pretty sure my heart holds its breath if only for a moment...

And I leap (expecting the descent to swallow me up...resigned to any outcome).

And suddenly, as if by spontaneous, Divine intervention, two wings appear at my side...MINE!

And I swiftly learn the rhythm and melody of flight up, down, up, down...And a whole orchestra plays along! The percussion, the trumpets, the flutes, the saxophones...all lifting me in song!

"I'm doing it!"

And it's so freakin' scary.

And I'm doing it.

I'm doing it.

I'm crossing the ocean. Fear and all.

And I'm looking back, only to take your hand to join me.

It's Time To Trade in My Tiara

One of the best things about growing older is the Noticing.

At some point, I Noticed Time slipping by like sand through an hour glass and realized, for goodness sake, I can't make everyone happy even if I try.

I noticed the risk of haemorrhaging for everyone else and decided to give blood discriminately instead.

Giving Life Blood is exactly what I tell myself I am doing when I am playing the role of Ms. Merry Martyr.

Somehow I convince myself that I alone can make everything and everyone alright.

In my Fairy Godmother garb, (complete with sparkly magic wand), right out of the Cinderella story, I know exactly what everyone wants and needs, and believe I alone have the power to give it to them.

(Of course, I am never robbing anyone of their free will or an opportunity to grow into their own power.)

You see, martyrdom has been modelled for me my entire life by the people I most admire.

Gina Hatzis

Being seen as a Good Girl was my most noble aspiration.

The problem is, this achievement hollowed me out and left me for dead.

My Life Blood had been drained from me and no external intravenous could replenish my soul.

And I noticed that I could actually take a break from saving the world. (gasp)

Heck, they don't really need me anyway.

And I also Noticed that I could spend my precious time and blood, saving myself instead.

Now I know, I know , Dear Dying Culture, that according to you, the most I can ever be and the highest I can ever aspire to, is showing up as A Woman of Servitude.

A kind, noble, pretty, quiet, sexy (when appropriate), motherly (at dinner time), generous (to the point of empty) kind-of-woman.

But Darlings,

I'm trading in my tiara for bedazzled horns.

I Want to Eat The Apple to the Core

One of my Too Much traits is INTENSITY.

I'm a Deep Dive kinda gal.

Screw the pleasantries and formal bios.

Fuck the weather and "how was your weekend?" conversation.

I wanna jump into your skin.

I want a glimpse into your soul.

I want to peek behind the mask, to witness your exhale, to hold space for your shoulders to soften.

I hold the preciousness of time in my small hands and know there isn't a moment to lose.

Now, this can be very intimidating in a world where pretense is the fashion du jour.

And I'll be the first to say I don't practice this with Every Person – Discernment is Key.

It takes intention, time, energy and a willingness to also put some skin in the game.

But I want to live the DEPTH of my life…Not just the width of it.

I want to eat the apple to the core, not just take a bite.

I want the whole meal, not just the samples from Costco.

Ya can't get full on the crumbs, Baby.

Be The Other Kind

"If you want the girl next door, go next door." – Joan Crawford

I've never been Her – the Girl Next Door – in my bones. Never.

I've always been the Other Kind.

The wild one. The untamed girl. The rebel. The black sheep. The ruffler of feathers. The odd one out. The weirdo.

For years I felt I should apologize for this.

Or feel guilty, ashamed, embarrassed.

Or compensate for it with responsibility, kindness, success and selflessness.

So I pretended I was her.

I dimmed down. Way down.

Until my light was almost imperceptible.

So faint, it didn't serve its purpose at all.

After all, what's the point of a light if not to illuminate?

And ultimately, I became Her.

That Girl Everyone Loves.

Predictable. Tame. Apologetic. Selfless.

Addicted to Servitude to find her worth.

The Martyr who died on the cross.

Nameless. Ambiguous. Bland.

So invisible I didn't see my own reflection in the mirror.

Thank goodness, I broke out of that trance.

But, I do often wonder who this Girl Next Door really is?

And why she gets so much damn attention anyway?

Is she even worth the fuss?

If I had to guess…she's probably inside scarfing down chocolates or binge drinking.

Peeking through the curtains wishing she could escape.

And be anywhere else,

Anyone else but the Girl Next Door.

Good Isn't So Great

When I examine my life, I realize all I really wanted to Be was Good.

It was the safest, most sure-fire way to lock down love and security, and subconsciously, that's all the 6 year-old in me desperately longed for.

But the quest for Good had led me so far from myself, I barely recognized my reflection anymore.

It didn't payout when I went to cash in my chips and it never wanted to snuggle after it had its way with me.

Truth is, I've outgrown Good.

Good is the skinny jeans from last season that never really fit quite right that had my Truth spilling over the edges like some unsightly muffin top.

Good had me crafting words and stories and a narrative that didn't represent me, like the smooth lines of a politician lying through gleaming white teeth.

Good made me afraid of myself, and my feelings and my desires.

GINA HATZIS

Good is Shame and Guilt and Conformity in drag.

A wolf in sheep's clothing.

Good never got me anywhere.

Except lost. And fragmented.

Good isn't admirable if it's a lie.

Not if it bows to fear and judgment and smallness.

Good doesn't always shine. Or radiate. Or glow.

Good doesn't know its power.

It doesn't sense its inherent worthiness.

It hasn't made friends with self-respect.

Good can only take you so far, to the limits of Acceptable, before you run into Truth.

And Truth, well, Truth is Who You Are.

And no matter how long you've been hiding from Her in the land of Good, Truth is gonna find you.

And she's gonna set you free.

I've Got This Covered

I've got my own back.

In the morning I rise.

Two feet over the side of the bed planted firmly. Balanced and ready to move Forward.

Two eyes squinting open, choosing what to See, what truths to focus on and when to look away.

One mind flooded with reality and circumstance ...so many decisions about Who to Be, What kind of day I will have and How I will show up in the world.

A spine that either bends over with regret and defeat, or straightens with Resilience and Resolve.

Two hands that clench and grab, or fold and pray.

One heart that hides and retracts in fear or opens and expands with love and willingness.

Choices. Always choices.

It's so wonderful to have the love and support of so many.

Thank you.

And yet, it's powerful to know that regardless, I have MY OWN BACK.

It begins here for me.

Energy Doesn't Lie

Stop Speaking. Your energy tells me all I need to know.

Do ya feel it?

Have you ever met someone and instantly felt a connection? Their vibe felt familiar, honest, resonant and you just like being in their presence?

And have you ever come across someone who says all the 'right' things and seems really popular and pleasant, but SOMETHING inside you just feels "off" around them?

That's energy.

Don't question it.

Your intuitive frequency picks up messages your senses can't catch up with.

There is an all-powerful force within that vibrates higher than your conscious awareness.

Trust it.

Energy never lies.

Ever.

Where The Divine Lives

Desire is where the Divine lives.

I have spent all day so far playing in my Sandbox... building castles and making plans.

And the theme that keeps coming up is Pleasure.

So many of us are disconnected from our Joy, our Juice, our G-Spot.

With how our Soul gets lit up and our Spirit comes alive.

We get into a rhythm of complacency, get comfortable in our personal corset of discomfort... acclimatized to an "okay" life and a "meh" existence.

This is not the dream the Universe has for you!

You are a spark of the Infinite, intended to experience waves of ecstasy, joy and bliss!

Not just on the weekend or on vacation or when you retire.

But every day. Endlessly. Repeatedly.

It begins with Knowing what you Desire...

And goes beyond a cleaning lady, a day at the spa or a win for your favourite team.

What do you Truly Desire?

Start a list and let 'er rip.

Be unrealistic.

Go beyond what's plausible or reasonable or even 'spiritual'.

Go hog wild! Big. Small. Ludicrous. Ridiculous. No judgment here. Want it. Want it all.

Allow yourself space to dream it.

Marinate in it.

Lust for it.

Imagine it.

Taste it.

Feel it.

This is the magic that was intended for your life.

The Divine lives in your Desire.

It expresses itself through your ecstasy and bliss.

Please, don't deny your Divinity.

Leaving Behind Your Clutter

A good friend of mine just moved into her beautiful new home.

As she gave me a tour, I marvelled at the clutterless-ness of each room.

So spacious and clean and unfettered.

She remarked that they left much behind and were very selective about what to bring into their new space.

Embarking on a New Year has me loving that.

Now I may not be moving any time soon, so any 'crap cleanse' may not be as easy, but I am very inspired to clear space In My Life for less.

And I'm not just talking about stuff either.

Less obstacles.
Less distraction.
Less noise.
Less mental clutter.
Less drama.
Less pressure.
Less facade.

Gina Hatzis

Less pretending.
Less pleasing and othering and random peopling.

I'm SO ready to let go of all the stuff clogging up my ease and breath and peace of mind.

To release myself from the shackles of Who I Should Be, and feel the weightlessness of sweet release as I rise in Who I Am.

What will you leave behind?

The Universe Loves A Mule
I fall. I fail. I trip, stumble, crumble.

I cry, throw my hands up in despair and growl at myself in the mirror.

I rant and rave and shout profanities to the wind because it feels so damn good.

I binge eat, starve myself, don't sleep, sleep too much.

I over-think, over-analyze and over-do everything.

I crumple myself up like a piece of paper and moan into my pillow.

And then...

And then...

I unfold myself.

I stand up.

Ball my fists.

Assume the warrior pose.

Breathe.

Focus my gaze.

Dig deep.

Deeper.

Deeper still.

I find that space in me where resilience lives.

I find that space in me that knows how to bend and not break.

I find that space in me that is pure Source energy.

And I get back to the business at hand…

Trusting the Magic to happen.

Knowing the Universe always fall madly in love with a stubborn mule.

Make Your Own Luck

On the Greek side of my family, we have a New Year's Day custom.

A delicious sweet bread is made and just before baking it, a coin is hidden inside the dough.

The family then gathers and as slices are cut, each member is named.

The person with the coin in their slice is supposed to have a lucky year.

Well this past year, I won. Not once, but twice – at two family events.

Now I'm hardly superstitious and I don't need a coin to predict my year.

Because when it comes to Luck, I don't wait for it or wish for it, I Cultivate It.

People always tell me that I'm lucky...

Yeah, if by "lucky" you mean...

Focused.

Celebrating the TOO MUCH WOMAN

Resilient.

Scared Shitless but Still Unstoppable.

Relentless.

Idealistic.

Passionate as Fuck.

Indestructible.

Aligned.

Conscious.

Hopeful.

Aware.

In the flow.

Open to learning.

Trusting the Universe.

Then yup....I'm lucky.

I knead my own dough, hide my own coin and then eat the Whole Damn Loaf in my life.

Knowing the "lucky coin" is in there somewhere and I will find it...if I just stay hungry.

Will this be your "lucky" year?

You decide...

Watch Out For Saboteurs and Press On
As you're on a mission to be the best version of yourself, adopt new habits or shine your light, please watch out for saboteurs.

These are the people in your life who want SO MUCH to love you, and yet, get stuck in the web of their own discomfort.

These characters come dressed as friends, spouses, siblings, parents, co-workers who "have your best interest at heart" and just want to point out the ridiculousness of your goal.

What to do?

Step 1. Thank them for their concern.
Step 2. Bless them so they may find peace within themselves.
Step 3. Put your blinders on. Keep moving.

Don't be bitter or angry or hurt.

Have compassion for the difficult space they're in where...

Your Fire Has Become a Mirror...reflecting back to them a wound of disappointment, fear and lack.

Decide the best way to respond is to be a loving example of what IS possible.

Send them love.

Ground yourself.

And onward, Baby!

Fall In Love With You

I'm a Lover.

There's no denying it.

I loooooove Love.

Giving it, oozing it, indulging in it, making it, writing, singing and daydreaming about it, even romanticising it.

There is nothing like the softness of my child's skin, the spark of a lightning kiss on my lips or the heart swell that occurs when I have connected deeply with another Soul friend.

However, for much of my life, love only showed up for me in OTHER-ing.

It required someone ELSE to catch the ball, someone ELSE to lead the tango, someone ELSE to balance the see-saw of my worth.

And there is frankly nothing, nada, zilch that replaces THAT. Connection is wired so deeply into the cellular makeup of humanity that we wither and die without it.

And yet, and yet, and yet, I have found that, like a recipe for my favourite dish, the order of ingredients makes a huge difference.

Gina Hatzis

If I come to love with another and I am barren within, I show up with an energy of desperation and fear, suffocating the flow of reciprocity that wants to flow like a waterfall, unconstrained and relaxed.

If I come to love filled with my own Life Force Vitality, awakened to my own worthiness and turned on by my own sense of aliveness, I show up with an energy of exuberance and magnetism. And love can't resist my offer to dance in musical ecstasy.

Taking time to date myself.
To romance myself.
To get curious about myself.

To wink at my reflection in the mirror and flirt with the Goddess within, has shifted how I show up.

Neediness replaced by confidence.

Desire displaced by radiance.

Grasping succeeded by honouring.

Create space to fall madly in love with you.

Trust me. You're the One.

You Can't Rush Magic

I'm Snailing it!

It's not how fast you go. Just go.

My Ego is infatuated with finish lines.

It's obsessed with crossing them – quickly and mercilessly.

It doesn't care about bloodied knees or broken bones, or my over-exerted heart, no.

It just wants to finish.

Check. Done. Sign. Sealed. Delivered.

But as I enter this race of life, I have come to see that all things unfold in Divine Timing, not according to how hard I run.

Like a baby in utero, requiring time for all the connective tissues of its miracle to develop just so, there's just no rushing the birth of magic.

Whatever possibility you are pregnant with, whatever dream of yours is swelling in your soul, honour the gestation period.

Allow for all of its tiny parts to fill in and catch up and mature just so.

Don't rush the miracle.

Its due date should not be the focus of your obsession.

Instead, become preoccupied with the process, become infatuated with the joy of anticipation and most of all, Darling, marinate in the absolute knowing that the birth of this dream that was seeded in you, is imminent.

It may not come as fast as you'd like or progress as quickly as you'd hoped.

But Baby, stay committed and rooted in faith.

Stay the course...no matter how slow your pace.

It may take time.

But you will snail it.

Be Your Own Sun

"You're your own sun."
What does that mean to you?

Your unique light – the Who of Who You Are – is a renewable Light.

It is self-sustaining, self-generating, brilliant and bright.

It requires nothing outside of you to shine its brilliance.

Not permission

Not approval

Not appreciation

Not even a recipient!

Oh! The years wasted trying to direct my shine like a flashlight so they would notice! So they would validate me. So, they could anoint me worthy.

The energy spent on chasing the dark in order to prove the magnificence of my light!

I see so many of you effort-ing. Telling me you're "getting there" or "not there yet" or hoping to have my 'this or that'.

You're the freaking SUN, dang it!

Own this! And if that's too far, let's play pretend like kids and imagine it. What would that feel like to know you ARE THE SUN?

When I'm glowing in the vibration of this knowing, everything becomes dewy and sparkly and yes, unicorns gallop by farting rainbows! You should see them!

I am the freaking sun.

and so are you.

And we require nothing – not a thing – outside of us to shine.

Not a witness, a like, a lover, a book deal, a win, a stage, a shit ton of money, not beauty, not success, not a freaking viral video. (although that was fun!)

Nada.

Shine on, Baby. Not for adoration.

Shine. Because you just can't dim the sun.

Waiting Through the Winter

I'm in the Winter of my life.

Day dreaming of Spring's cherry blossoms

And licking Summer ice cream drips from a cone.

Craving the crunch of Autumn leaves and the smell of apple pie wafting up my nose.

But it's Winter in my Soul.

I'm wrapped in a blanket of desire...a straitjacket of impatience.

I warm my toes bedside a fire whose flickering flames taunt me like a seductive belly dancer.

Wooing me to "...come closer, closer, just a little closer, dear" until the burn of reality scalds my awakened senses.

"Patience!" She hisses – frustrated with my naiveté and immaturity.

"Patience." She whispers again. Gently this time, sympathetic to my longing.

"Patience, Darling." Coddling me now. Worried I may not hold out much longer.

So I sit in my Winter.

I acclimatize to the shivering, rhythmic music of the season's song.

I hum a tune a friend once sang in my ear.

I...am...patient
I...am...patient
I...am...patient

Repeating like a mantra, skipping like a record, over and over and over again until my body is warm under the coals of my strength.

I'm in the winter of my life and I'm okay holding on.

No winter lasts forever.

Spring is silently preparing her grand arrival

The Wild Path

"Of all the paths you take in life, make sure a few are dirt."
–John Muir

I have followed the paved road

The easy road

The well-lit road

And the yellow brick road.

I have played it safe.

Very safe.

Too safe.

And it wasn't until I decided to off-road...

To risk the road less travelled...

To trust the dirt path

That I finally found my way.

The views aren't always scenic, (and ya need a dang good bra to safely navigate those bumps!) and yet my soul knows that this is where it needs to go.

GINA HATZIS

Climbing over and through, dirt under my nails and burrs in my wild hair, jeans ripped at the knees and the where-to-pee panic.

Sunlight playing peek-a-boo through the trees and smells taunt the savage in me.

Grunting, moaning, howling in unison with my wolf pack.

This is living.

Wild, unrestrained, free.

Staying With Your Present Self

> "What matters is not just that this happened,
> but who I will become because it did.
> Dear God let my suffering not have been in vain.
> Let me become a women so kick-ass fabulous,
> wise, compassionate, strong, amazing,
> because I went through this."
> –Marianne Williamson.

This past year or two has shattered me.

Oh no! Don't be sorry. See, I asked for this.

In August of 2016, I asked to be used to live and serve at my Highest capacity.

I'm an all-in kinda gal. I don't, can't, won't half-ass my life.

The urgency to fulfil my potential in this lifetime was alive in me from my earliest childhood recollection.

At every painful turn, I have been present with two levels of awareness.

The first, was my present body experience. What was actually happening in real time.

The second, was a parallel but detached awareness (I called it my Future Self until I learned quantum theory), that watched my other self with compassion, perspective, reverence and love.

It is ALL part of the master plan. To ready me and evolve my soul to serve.

Nothing in vain. And yet, I am undeniably human – flesh and blood.

And it is normal, safe and expected that I FEEL into each experience and not bypass it with shame, guilt or in the spirit of 'moving on'...

Suffering allows for contrast.

Contrast offers clarity.

Clarity brings awareness.

Awareness invites growth.

Growth is the very definition of Life.

So I honour it all.

If this is where you're at Darling, breathe into the present.

It's a sacred sliver of time that requires your full embodiment so that you can transcend this level of awareness and ascend to your Highest Self.

You are more powerful than you know.

And your healing serves a purpose greater than you.

We all ask you to do what needs to be done, to take the time required, to be intentional with the alchemy of your medicine.

It will serve the world.

And on behalf of all us, past, present and future,

Thank you.

It's Not About Saying the Popular Thing

The lion and tiger may be more powerful, but the wolf does not perform in the circus.

The lone wolf.

That's me.

I don't always say the popular thing.

I shy away from the masses and their herd mentality.

And I won't...I can't just stick around and play games with those who won't take responsibility for themselves.

I refuse to be a doormat. A scapegoat. A push over.

A wolf protects her energy and honours her sacred heart.

A wolf won't hang around and fight an unnecessary scrap.

She won't play circus games and blame others for who they are.

She refuses to dance in circles of gossip, judgment or shame.

GINA HATZIS

A wolf will pause

Gather herself

Raise her head
Perk up her ears

Even if she walks alone

A wolf is not meant for the circus. She is wild and fierce and has shit to do.

I am a wolf.

You Know You're A Miracle, Right?

If you don't believe in miracles, perhaps you have forgotten you are one.

Think back: At what age did you decide that you weren't a miracle or that miraculous things couldn't happen?

At what point did the magic start to dissipate?

When a crawling ant or airplane in the sky no longer stopped you in your tracks to gawk with awe and wonder?

When did you no longer marvel at the way your body could move and dance and jump and run?

Or stare at yourself in mirror with adoring self-love...

How long ago did the music of your dreams fade and remix into a track of reason, logic and practicality?

Making transitions like a skilled DJ- so smooth and subtle- you probably thought it was maturity talking?

And what will it take...
What
Will
It

Take
to remind you, awaken you, to the truth of your Miraculous Self?

Illness? Divorce? Loss? Failure? Success? The moment of clarity before Death?

Look around at the majesty of your life:

In nature.

In the eyes of someone you love.

In the mirror.

Remember who you are.

Remember what you are.

You ARE a Miracle.

Now go astonish yourself.

My Own Shot of Whiskey

I am so grateful to the Haters and Naysayers.

It's painful to admit that often times the people closest to you are the ones holding you back from your greatest potential.

I see every single person that shows up in my life as an integral player supporting my growth and fullest expression.

But I am also aware that, in the play of my life, the characters in each scene are given different roles.

Some do it with kind words and big ears and warm arms.

Some do it by popping up and cheering from the side-lines – pompoms shaking and pure love chants.

And still others support my growth by being the Naysayers.

By playing small themselves.

By taunting my Ego with words and actions that invite me to shrink from my greatness.

By challenging my sense of Enough-ness.

By threatening my faith and choking my spirit.

Challenging me to break out from my cocoon of small-mindedness, comfort and fear.

In some ways, these are the most significant characters in my story.

They don't coddle me or love me unconditionally or make it all okay.

Sometimes, they don't even hang around long enough to pretend to care.

Unknowingly, they wrap me so tightly in their stranglehold of judgment and self-loathing...that I have no choice but to fight back and bust through and beyond their once impenetrable fortress.

And I am free. It surprises us both as I flit away with my new found wings.

Off to find my Tribe. My Soul Tribe who celebrate my arrival.

I am forever grateful for you.

For all of you – whichever role you play.

It's all perfect.

After all, I'd rather be my own shot of whiskey than everyone's cup of tea.

Let's Do Abso-fricken-lutely Nothing To day

Let's stop the Glorification of Busy

Let's make a deal.

Let's agree to stop celebrating our busyness.

Let's agree that slow is best, it's desirable, it's even sexy.

Let's cheer for one another when we take a break, have a nap or 'waste' our time.

Let's high-five a friend who DIDN'T hustle to get shit done and let's congratulate her on taking a long luxurious bath instead.

Let's brag about lounging on the couch and not accomplishing anything at all while the laundry and dishes pile up.

Let's laugh about our full schedules and how everything can just freaking wait.

Let's ignore the need to accomplish things and check boxes on our To Do List to prove our worthiness.

Let's be bold and daring Baby, and dig our heels into RECEIVING today.

And just do abso-fricken-lutely NOTHING but live in this exquisite moment.

And celebrate that.

Because we are Human BEINGS first and foremost.

And life is for the Living.

I Am Responsible for This One Life

No matter your spiritual or pragmatic beliefs about why we're here, we can all agree that each of us was individually gifted a life.

I have mine. And you, yours.

And when that fateful days comes, and we each take our last breaths, we will face the reckoning of our decisions.

The good, the bad and the what-the-frick-was-I-thinking?

I will not blame Charlie or the weather or the economy or my parents or aliens for how my life was lived.

It won't matter who was in office or the crappy genetic cards I was dealt or even the thickness of my thighs.

I will stand in the Knowing that I was responsible for the energy I brought to each moment, for the choices I ultimately made, and how many times I let Fear or Love drive the car.

It's all on me.

Me.

And I accept that wholeheartedly (albeit with shaky knees), because that gives me full permission to live my life.

Not according to standards.

Not according to expectations.

Not according the way the wind blows on any given day.

And certainly not according to what anyone else believes is best for me.

My life.

Mine.

I claim it.

And the good news Baby, is you get to have yours.

I Came Here To Play

Dare to Suck!

The #1 and #2 challenges I hear about in my work is Fear of Failure and lacking the Courage to Leap in the first place.

We are so programmed to receive the check mark, the accolade, the rave review, that we lack the fortitude to risk anything.

What if it sucks? What if no one likes it?

What if I put my heart and soul on a platter and nobody comes to the table? Or worse, what if they take a bite and spit it out?

Yeah, what if?

Look. I'm a hard core recovering Perfectionist.

I have left more magic undone in me then I care to admit.

I have sat on the side-lines watching other people play the Game of Life, heart in my hands, aching to get on the field and just Try for many seasons.

And as I've sat there, eating my Popcorn of Regret, I have missed out on so much opportunity.

Gina Hatzis

Not just the chance to win, (yeah we all want that), but the chance to be In The Game.

To feel electricity shoot down my legs, my heart pump with exhilaration, my hands clammy with expectation, and my spirit alive with possibility!

To have my knees bloodied and my shirt muddied, and the tears of my humanity stain my cheeks.

To be willing to suck, yeah, actually suck, so that my soul might taste the glory of Playing.

If we are smart, we can convince ourselves that 'this is as good as it gets' and there is no need to stretch beyond our comfort zone.

If we are really smart, we know there is always more waiting for us, and sometimes we need to trust that the fall is a necessary part of the flight.

And perhaps simply getting in the Game is the Win.

So, I'm deciding to Play, regardless of outcome.

Go ahead Universe.

Flick me off the edge.

I'm game.

Maybe the Moon Marvels at You

Last night, at 1:11am, the moon woke me up for a date.

I marvelled at her utter beauty.

She serenaded me with a love song, spoiled me with kisses and as her moonlight bathed my body in a blanket of Light, she disappeared behind the clouds.

She left me glowing, marinating in a splendour of wonder and awe.

I thought for a moment that it all might fade now that she was gone...

But it didn't.

The glow remained.

And I began to wonder, if perhaps I was the Source of that magnificent Light?

Was the magic I felt originating within ME?

And maybe it was the moon that came out to marvel at MY beauty instead?

Show Up in The Fullness of You

"To avoid criticism. Say nothing. Do nothing. Be nothing."
– Elbert Hubbard

There is nothing more confronting for a recovering People Pleaser than to Show Up Fully exposed.

Like an artist unveiling their masterpiece.

A musician sharing a personal melody.

A stripper baring her skin.

It's all out there.

Unmasked.

Unprotected.

Unsafe.

Allowing, inviting, and perhaps even daring the audience to judge the offering.

The unspoken question, "Do you like it?" hanging heavy in the air like lingerie on a clothesline.

Delicate.

Vulnerable.

Susceptible to the 'yeas' and 'nays' of the breeze that blows.

Praise from the East.

Criticism from the West.

Gripping the line with white knuckles and praying the storm clouds pass by.

What's the alternative?

To sit – a wet heap in a corner – rotting away in fear, self-loathing and resentment.

To disappear like a honeymoon negligee, continually pushed to the back of the drawer.

Further and further into the recesses of once-upon-a-time.

Forgotten. Purposeless.

Not I. No, not I.

Show up, my love, show up.

Let us see you in the fullness that you are.

We are all waiting for you.

Dare to Be Seen

Dare to be seen in all your Glory!

What is more important than being Seen?

I make the case for 'Nothing'.

It's even more important than being beautiful, being right, being successful, being the best, being perfect and even more important than being adored.

When someone Sees you with Intention, they don't impose their stuff on you or try to make it better.

There is no judgment or rationalization or need to explain.

When you are Seen, you can laugh loudly with no need to cover your mouth.

When you are Seen, you can weep and moan in sadness without needing to explain or pull yourself together.

When you are truly Seen...

the love handles and scars,
the greys and the bags under the eyes,
the fears and vulnerabilities

are transmuted into golden flecks of deep reverence for your Truth.

When you are Truly Seen,
And they don't flinch...

That is magic right there.

Here's lookin' at YOU, kid

I see you.
And I love what I see

I Wish You Courage

As I sink into my heartfelt dream for you from the infinite field of possibility, I can distill it all down to One Wish.

I wish you Courage.

May Courage shoot like lightening down your legs and give you the strength to walk towards your dreams.

May Courage rumble deep in your belly, the seat of your intuition, and give you the faith to listen to your inner guidance.

May Courage swell in your heart and give you the audacity to love in the face of fear and doubt.

May Courage broaden your shoulders so you have the power to stand tall in your Truth.

May Courage hold up your chin so you can be bold in your desire and know you are worthy of everything.

May Courage fill your mouth so you can let truth spill from your trembling lips.

May Courage pool in your eyes so you can see beyond the obstacles and have vision for your possibilities.

May Courage wrap itself like a halo around your head so you feel the support of the Universe and know you don't have to figure this out alone.

And most of all Darling, may Courage bud like Angel's Wings behind you, lifting you up, higher than ever before, into your most Glorious Self.

This is my wish for you.

In complete awe and adoration of all that you are.

Finding My Spiritual G Spot

Now that I've started, I just can't stop!

Here is the introduction to my next book, *Finding My Spiritual G Spot*.

Coming soon! Stay tuned for more…

Spiritual G Spot is a RECLAMATION.

A REcovery.

A REposession.

A REtrieval.

A REdemption.

A REsuscitation.

Ultimately, it's a REgrouping of all the slices of a Soul that come apart over the course of her lifetime –whether by chance or by choice, in stages or in an instant, thoughtfully or unintentionally.

It's about wholeness and integration. It's about irony and truth.

It's about embracing the blurred lines and oxymoronic labels of Who We Are in any given moment.

It's about Choice. Lots of it. And exploring the width and depth and breadth of the possibilities available to us as we attempt to sculpt an answer to the age old question, "Who Am I and Why Am I Here, anyway?"

This book is my bold, albeit messy, attempt at Courage.

I'm a woman who wants to be seen. I'm also a woman who has suffered the repercussions of being seen, and who has consequently dimmed the essence of my Light as a means of self-protection and self-preservation.

I'm a woman who has made a bold decision to show up anyway at the intersection of Too Much and Not Enough Street, because what I firmly believe is that **invisibility suffocates the Soul.**

WITH HEARTFELT THANKS

I need to begin with my mother Mary Ann, who has always encouraged and celebrated my Too Muchness. I have always known I was loved by you, and you will always be home to me. Truly the Wind Beneath my Wings.

To my children Antonio and Isabella, thank you for choosing me, for inspiring me, for teaching me and for encouraging me to live my truth, knowing that the greatest gift I can give to you is a happy mother.

To Anicio for your unwavering support for all of my wild escapades, for being a solid anchor and most of all, for the gift of our beautiful children.

To my stepfather George, you came and loved me as a father should. I am forever grateful for you in my life. Love you More.

To my brother Tony, the best big brother a girl could ask for. Having you in my corner makes me feel invincible. And yes, let's never mention you locking me in the suitcase again.

To my new little brother Anton, for showing up as proof that miracles can happen.

Celebrating the TOO MUCH WOMAN

To my father Ted, you have influenced the woman I am more than you know. I will always love you and hold a place for you in my life.

To my prima Mary, the sister I always wanted, and Marty my constant b.f.f., for cheering for my success and really meaning it.

To my incredible team: My editor Patti, I consider you proof that the universe is conspiring in my favour, Lee for being my technical saviour, treasured confidant and coach, Luckey for your endless enthusiastic yeses, to Claralynn for taking care of every loose end, and to Gabrial for your spiritual guidance and business coordination, for showing me angels do exist and for my very own song.

To Rina for the nachos, the laughs and for helping to ignite the Movement, and Dan, the co-host of SpeakerSlam, for creating the platform for the Too Much Woman to be birthed.

To Goalcast for continuing to share my work globally.

To the Too Much Women leaders who have come forward to host events to support the tour, and those who travel to meet me, you will always hold a special place in my heart. I pass the torch to you.

To Liz Dawn Donahue for the opportunity to speak alongside my mentors at the Woman's International Summit and launch this book, and for affirming my worth in such a big way.

To the millions of women (and men) who have watched my video and shared it, who have reached out with love and in solidarity, who have bared their souls, thank you for reminding me are never alone.

And lastly, my love and gratitude to the beautiful souls in my Facebook community. Oh! I have such immense love for you! Without your kind words, your courageous sharing, your enduring loyalty, this book would not exist.

About the Author

A recovering journalist, Gina is celebrating over 24 years as an International Corporate and Public Speaker, specializing in stellar communications, leadership and personal empowerment.

She is a blogger, writer, spoken word artist and the host of her podcast Spiritual G Spot, broadcasting in over 70 countries worldwide.

Gina has two viral videos amassing over 25 million views and is currently on a global tour as the visionary of the Too Much Woman Movement, a platform for women to shine fully in their unique glory.

When she's not speaking, writing, dancing or singing carpool karaoke, she is mothering her amazing teenagers in Toronto, Canada, and trying desperately to convince them she is still ⌧dope⌧.

This is her first book. Her second, Finding My Spiritual G Spot, is being birthed.

You can connect with Gina here:

www.ginahatzis.com

https://www.facebook.com/Gina.TooMuchWoman/?tn-str=k*F

www.Instagram.com/GinaHatzis

https://www.youtube.com/channel/ UCwXwYj8eUkemV34b0ItSm6w

https://ca.linkedin.com/in/gina-hatzis-3611aa8b

Celebrating the TOO MUCH WOMAN

To see this piece performed in its original format, visit my Facebook page at Gina Hatzis ⊠Too Much Woman:

https://www.facebook.com/Gina.TooMuchWoman/

videos/2044696289118780/

or on my YouTube channel

https://youtu.be/IQ-AfUz3g4I

To check out the edited Goalcast version that went viral, go here:

https://www.facebook.com/dailygoalcast/

videos/1806232156112505/

www.ingramcontent.com/pod-product-compliance
Lightning Source LLC
Chambersburg PA
CBHW071347290426
44108CB00014B/1462